The Reason for Joy

James E. Duncan, Jr.

BROADMAN PRESS

Nashville, Tennessee

To Bill, Kim, Gena, and Kathy

my super-grace children

Dewey Decimal Classification: 234.1
Subject headings: GRACE // THEOLOGY // CHRISTIAN LIFE
Library of Congress Catalog Card Number: 77-78470
Printed in the United States of America

Foreword

From the moment of salvation, every believer has eternal security and the potential for maximum happiness in this lifetime. God provided for this before the foundation of the world with his pre-designed plan called *grace*. God gave each of us volition. We will be either positive or negative toward his plan.

What a joy and blessing it has been to learn the full meaning of grace. Our attitude has changed from one of working for God to relaxing and letting God work in and through us. We no longer attempt to live the Christian life for him in our own strength through church activities and religious functions. Instead, we allow God to be our strength through acknowledging his presence in us, yielding in availability to him, and constantly remembering what we know about him, moment by moment and situation by situation. As a result, all of our activities and ministries can be a positive demonstration of the miraculous Christian life.

Our relationships, routines, and responsibilities have taken on new meaning under James E. Duncan, Jr.'s living and teaching grace principles. We know, now, that nothing can defeat us when we allow the indwelling Holy Spirit to control us. The problems we face daily may not change or be removed, but the key is having a relaxed mental attitude toward them. This can be done by consistent intake and daily application of Bible promises.

THE REASON FOR JOY defines the concepts of God's grace and will give you some helpful mechanics for living this victorious, stabilized, and joyous life which depends totally on him and never on us. In these pages, you will discover that God has made adequate provision for every phase of life and for all eternity.

You will learn that God is just waiting for you to live by faith, in order that he might give you the capacity to receive all that he has provided.

We believe that as you read this book with a positive attitude and apply the principles set forth, you, too, will experience freedom and enjoy life to its fullest, realizing that God has already provided everything you need. Truly, God's grace is sufficient.

WAYNE AND DORIS HAMMIT

Contents

Acknowledgments

My thanks and sincere appreciation are extended to my lovely wife, Ruth, for typing and proofing this manuscript. In addition, the encouragement from the deacons of the Dale City Baptist Church was used as a grace provision from God to provide the endurance needed to complete this endeavor.

Unless otherwise indicated, all Scripture quotations are from the Amplified Bible.

Introduction

God has a world of wealth and wisdom waiting for willing minds to want. These spiritual wonders are wrapped up in his written Word. Thus, in the Scriptures, God has made known his ability for our acquittal from sin. His revelation for our restoration is in the gospel of Jesus Christ which is the power of God unto salvation.

In addition, God has revealed a way for believers to walk in spiritual vitality and victory every day. Thus, we have much more than salvation. All through life we can abide in absolute assurance against the allurements and the aggressive acts of evil. The fantastic formula that opens the door to this fortress of God's faithfulness is our faith in Jesus Christ.

Because of our faith in Jesus Christ and a positive availability to his Word, we can abound daily in the atmosphere of God's adequacy. We can celebrate our relationship with him in an attitude of appreciation. As a result, we will be aware of God's approval and acceptance. Yes, every area and aspect of satanic assaults can be arrested through dependence on Jesus Christ. In him we have an advocate with the Father. He is the founder and finisher of our faith.

"Looking away [from all that will distract] to Jesus, Who is the Leader *and* the Source of *our* faith [giving the first incentive for our belief] and is also its Finisher, [bringing it to maturity and perfection]. He, for the joy [of obtaining the prize] that was set before Him, endured the cross, despising *and* ignoring the shame, and is now seated at the right hand of the throne of God" (Heb. 12:2).

How can these consoling conclusions be calculated? They are gleaned as spiritual gems from the mind of the Master—the Bible. From a serious study of his precious promises, we can see that God has for us a glamorous garden of grandeur called *grace*. Within this spiritual garden, he has gathered all of his goodness which he is

7

qualified to give on the basis of the cross.

Thus, God's grace is that all-inclusive package of provisions which he has provided for our profit. This grace package represents God's unsearchable and unchangeable riches which he has made available at Christ's cost. They inculcate all the energy and exercises of the Godhead for salvation, for successful Christian living, and for security in eternity. These grace provisions are undeserved and unmerited. We can't earn, deserve, or work for them. Praise the Lord! We don't have to. In addition, they are unique in quality and unlimited in quantity.

What is the origin of God's grace-goodness? This grace package was perceived in the very mind of God the Father from eternity past. It was processed and perpetuated as the very purpose of God for all people. It became a reality for us through the reconciling work of our Redeemer on the cross and his resurrection from the dead. This means that long before the world began, God made available his adequacy for every problem, every pressure, and every prosperity we will ever encounter.

"To me, though I am the very least of all the saints (God's consecrated people), this grace (favor, privilege) was granted *and* graciously entrusted: to proclaim to the Gentiles the unending (boundless, fathomless, incalculable and exhaustless) riches of Christ—wealth which no human being could have searched out" (Eph. 3:8).

Consequently, it is my purpose in this book to spell out some of the glorious genius of God's grace. It is my desire to make the reader mindful of some of God's meaningful mechanics for living the Christian life. These heavenly handles can help us generate God's grace-goodness to the gloomy, grievous experiences of our everyday existence.

Furthermore, my prayer is that you will pull from these pages the fulfilling fact that as a believer in Jesus Christ, you have his presence and power related to your life in the person of the Holy Spirit. Also, I will challenge you to rejoice in the riches and realities of God's grace reserve. I will encourage you to release by faith-dependence his megaton might, that he is in you, moment by moment and situation by situation.

This is not wishful wanting. My thesis and my testimony are that we can have mental solace, satisfaction, and stability amid our daily dreads. We can find the faith that fulfills every longing for liberty. We can actually invoke the power of God that will divert the fiery darts of fear and failure. The key is to discover and release in our thinking some of these tremendous treasures of truth which we are privileged to possess in Christ Jesus.

Let us now venture into God's garden of grace wonders, which he has waiting for willing minds to want. From the first chapter on, we will amplify some exciting grace procedures which God has designed. They will introduce us to the vitality of life which accompanies the Holy Spirit's control. We will progress from the new birth, through the Christian's daily life, and on into that eternal day which will be dominated by the personal presence of Jesus, his perfect happiness, and God's perpetual newness.

As you make your pilgrimage through these pages, be prepared to pick up some powerful tools. These implements can increase your capacity to receive all God can pour out in and through you. As a result, you will not be plagued and spiritually paralyzed by those sin-nature flaws which can cause your faith to falter before the finish. Instead, you can know God's grace which is your *reason for joy*.

Part I
Grace for Salvation

We now come to the first stop on our journey through God's glorious garden of grace. We shall call this first area *Grace for Salvation*. Salvation grace is the sin solution for sinners, made available through Christ's activity on the cross. Included in this area is all that was needed for the personal restoration of mankind to a right relationship to God. In this division, we shall deal with the "Barricade Dilemma" and the "New Birth."

1

The Barricade Dilemma

Think of the breach between unsaved mankind and holy God as a roadway packed with barricades. Because of these obstructions, a right relationship and fulfilling fellowship with God were impossible. Furthermore, God demanded man's dedicated dependence and diligent devotion.

However, there was no possible procedure through which mankind, in his own strength, could break down or bypass these barricades. This meant that mankind was blocked from God, lost to his liberty, locked out of his love, and banished from his blessings. So, man was faced with a desperate dilemma. Somehow and in some way, the barricades had to be removed. "But your iniquities have made a separation between you and your God, and your sins have hid His face from you, so that He will not hear" (Isa. 59:2).

The Barricades Erected

How were these barricades built between God and mankind? This barricade dilemma existed because the first man, Adam, chose to heed Satan's deception. In the Garden of Eden, God provided perfectly, in grace, for Adam and Eve. But they deliberately decided to desert their right relationship with righteous God and moved out from under his management. They were no longer grateful for God's government nor agreeable to his guidance. So, they stepped out of dependence on God into independence from him.

"And when the woman saw that the tree was good (suitable and pleasant) for food, and that it was delightful to look at and a tree to be desired to make one wise, she took of its fruit and ate; and she gave some also to her husband, and he ate" (Gen. 3:6).

As a result, they died spiritually and became separated from God. This meant that they were only soulishly alive. They had lost their capacity to relate to God. Now, if this had been all that happened, mankind would have been harmless as a dove. But the act of man's mischief resulted in his receiving an anti-God sin nature. It is against God, incapable of pleasing him, and its thoughts and activities are unacceptable to him.

"[That is] because the mind of the flesh—with its carnal thoughts and purposes—is hostile to God; for it does not submit itself to God's Law, indeed it cannot. So then those who are living the life of the flesh—catering to the appetites and impulses of their carnal nature—cannot please *or* satisfy God, *or* be acceptable to Him (Rom. 8:7–8).

Being then independent of the Father, Adam and Eve became dependent on this sin principle, which constituted an intrusion into the plan of God for them.

In addition, another even more fatal consequence of Adam's course of action was that all creation would inherit this intrusion and be considered guilty before God. Thus, every person is possessed by this polluted lower nature. "Therefore as sin came into the world through one man and death as the result of sin, so death spread to all men, [no one being able to stop it *or* to escape its power] because all men sinned" (Rom. 5:12). This meant that, with this sin nature in man's mind, Satan now had a point of contact through which he could infiltrate his anti-God doctrines and concepts.

Satan had erected the barricades of sin between man and God. As a result, man was confined to the slave house of sin. He was without hope and void of God's happiness in time, with no possibility of heaven.

"As it is written, None is righteous, just *and* truthful *and* upright *and* conscientious, no, not one. No one understands—no one intelligently discerns *or* comprehends; no one seeks out God. All have turned aside; together they have gone wrong *and* have become unprofitable *and* worthless; no one does right, not even one!" (Rom. 3:10–12).

The Barricades Erased

Since man was powerless to proceed with any program of pleasing God, what could he do? Nothing! Absolutely nothing. Think of it! There was absolutely nothing man could do to remedy his predicament and remove the barriers. So, man was defeated with no defense against the deceptions of the devil and the depravity of the intrusion—his sin nature.

But there is a solution. Standing as a majestic mandate on Golgotha's hill is God's statue of liberty for the human race. It is the cross. It represents the death of man's Savior, Jesus Christ. On the cross of Calvary, God the Father accomplished for man what man couldn't achieve for himself. God removed the barricades. He made available for all people his righteous reprieve, his paid-for pardon, his adequate acquittal, and his formula for forgiveness. Jesus Christ is God's answer to man's dilemma. He is God's source for man's salvation, God's safety ground for sinners and God's seal for eternal security.

"Having cancelled *and* blotted out *and* wiped away the handwriting of the note (or bond) with its legal decrees *and* demands, which was in force *and* stood against us—hostile to us. This [note with its regulations, decrees and demands] He set aside *and* cleared completely out of our way by nailing it to [His] cross" (Col. 2:14).

What actually occurred on the cross? At this point in our journey, it is important to explore fully what was involved in God's removing this besetting blockade. The cross of Christ is more than a gimmick of self-hypnosis or a system for mental incantation to escape the pressures and problems of our spiritual warfare with sin. Nor is the purpose of the cross a way to merely seek an emotional stability amid a series of substitutes. Instead, the cross represents a definite, deliberate, divine work called grace. This work was done by God through Christ on man's behalf. We are calling the first stage, *Grace for Salvation.*

Now let us examine, on the basis of the Scriptures, the specific work which God wrought through Jesus Christ on the cross. We will review how he erased each barricade and thus renewed for man the possibility of the relationship which Adam ruined.

First Barricade—Slavery to Sin

"All have sinned and are falling short of the honor *and* glory which God bestows *and* receives" (Rom. 3:23).

The basis of this barricade is built on Adam's choice to live by his own convictions and conclusions instead of God's calling. As a result, mankind must go its own weak way of defeat. Unregenerate man knows nothing of God's mighty way of miraculous living. Because he fails to meet God's standard, man has no alternative but to go against God and follow the dictates of his sin nature. In addition, man can't break the hold of sin which has his soul in a straightjacket. Man is a helpless and hopeless victim of slavery to sin.

God erased this barricade through Christ's death on the cross. He purchased man's freedom from the slavery of sin. This is an essential part of God's salvation package which freed mankind from sin and provided an alternative to slavery. This means there is a doorway out of the slave house of sin. By faith, man can walk out into freedom.

"In Whom we have our redemption *through His blood,* [which means] the forgiveness of our sins" (Col. 1:14). "My little children, I write you these things so that you may not violate God's law *and* sin; but if any one should sin, we have an Advocate (One Who will intercede for us) with the Father; [it is] Jesus Christ [the all] righteous—upright, just, Who conforms to the Father's will in every purpose, thought and action" (1 John 2:1).

Beware! It is a terrible tragedy when, after liberation from sin's slavery, we live as if we were still there. This happens when believers fail to fill their minds with Bible knowledge and refuse to operate under the Holy Spirit's control.

Second Barricade—Separation

"As it is written, None is righteous, just *and* truthful *and* upright *and* conscientious, no, not one. No one understands—no one intelligently discerns *or* comprehends; no one seeks out God. All have turned aside; together they have gone wrong *and* have become unprofitable *and* worthless; no one does right, not even one!" (Rom. 3:10–12).

The concept in this barricade is that because of man's sin, he is separated (cut off) from God. This is what it means to be lost. It is spiritual death.

Therefore, God has an IOU against mankind. Man owes God love, obedience, and the keeping of all his laws. But man is incapable of paying his debt. Therefore, man can do nothing to nullify his separation.

Jesus erased this barricade through taking our place on the cross.

He paid in full God's just demands against us and satisfied him completely. He blotted out our sins. "Having cancelled *and* blotted out *and* wiped away the handwriting of the note (or bond) with its legal decrees *and* demands, which was in force *and* stood against us—hostile to us. This [note with its regulations, decrees and demands] He set aside *and* cleared completely out of our way by nailing it to [His] cross" (Col. 2:14).

Third Barricade—Death

"For the wages which sin pays is death; but the [bountiful] free gift of God is eternal life through (in union with) Jesus Christ our Lord" (Rom. 6:23).

This barricade is built on the fact that when we are born physically into the world, we are spiritually dead in sin. We are alive physically but dead spiritually. Furthermore, there is no way that man can remedy this dilemma. Thus, he can't change the spiritual death he acquired at physical birth.

God erased this barricade through providing a new birth. This means that because of the cross, a spiritual regeneration is available for every person. Spiritual birth overcomes the problem of physical birth. What Adam's sin lost, we can regain through the new birth. We can be born again and become spiritually alive in Jesus Christ.

By a play on words, we can learn that if we are born only once (physical birth), we will die twice, the physical death and the second death. If we are born twice, (the physical birth and the spiritual birth), we will die only once, the physical death which is a doorway into heaven to be with God forever.

"He came to that which belonged to Him—to His own [domain, creation, thing, world]—and they who were His own did not receive Him *and* did not welcome Him. But to as many as did receive *and* welcome Him, He gave the authority [power, privilege, right] to become the children of God, that is, to those who believe in—adhere to, trust in and rely on—His name" (John 1:11–12).

"Jesus answered him, I assure you, most solemnly I tell you, that unless a person is born again (anew, from above), he cannot ever see—know, be acquainted with [and experience]—the kingdom of God" (John 3:3).

Fourth Barricade—Sin Nature

"However, it is no longer I who do the deed, but the sin [principle] which is at home in me *and* has possession of me. For I know that nothing good dwells within me, that is, in my flesh. I can will what is right, but I cannot perform it.—I have the intention and urge to do what is right, but no power to carry it out" (Rom. 7:17–18).

The sin nature is a part of our lives because of Adam's sin. It produces personal sins which were paid for by Jesus' work on the cross. In addition, the sin nature produces relative goodness which was rejected by Jesus' work on the cross. Relative goodness means that man can be good when it is to his advantage to be good. We can do good deeds, hide bad features, and exhibit the appearance of sincerity. Because of the sin nature, man seeks to solve his problems, set up his own perfect environment, and saturate his life with the details of life as his source of happiness. But none of man's goodness is acceptable to God. God rejects everything that falls from the sin nature.

God erased this barricade through his forgiveness provided by Jesus Christ on the cross. His forgiveness was applied to our lives the moment we trusted him for salvation. Furthermore, when we believed in Christ, God credited to our lives his own goodness. Therefore, God accepts us, not because we are good or have earned anything from him but because we have his righteousness in our lives.

"All have sinned and are falling short of the honor *and* glory which God bestows *and* receives" (Rom. 3:23).

"For our sake He made Christ [virtually] to be sin Who knew no sin, so that in *and* through Him we might become [endued with, viewed as in and examples of] the righteousness of God—what we ought to be, approved and acceptable and in right relationship with Him, by His goodness" (2 Cor. 5:21).

Fifth Barricade—Sovereignty

"Whom God put forward [before the eyes of all] as a mercy seat *and* propitiation by His blood—the cleansing and life-giving sacrifice of atonement and reconciliation—[to be received] through faith. This was to show God's righteousness, because in His divine forbearance

He had passed over *and* ignored former sins without punishment"
(Rom. 3:25).

God's sovereignty signifies his total perfection which cannot sym-
pathize or socialize with evil. Because of Adam's sin, every soul is a
sinner separated from God. This means that before God's sin solution
could be served to sinners, his eternal essence had to be satisfied.
Because of man's sin nature, he cannot solve his separation from God.
In no way could man's self efforts and self-centered goodness satisfy
God's sovereignty and merit or master his salvation.

God erased this barricade on the cross because his love found a
formula to free him from his own right and just requirement. God
must be just and judge sin. However, he desired to distribute to
mankind his perfect love and liberating life. Since man couldn't solve
his separation from sovereignty, God's activity on the cross accomplished it for him. On the cross of Calvary, the righteous and just
demands of God were satisfied. Therefore, from the moment of
salvation, God can freely express his love to us. He also gives to us his
eternal life by way of his personal presence in the person of the Holy
Spirit and his written Word.

"And God purposed that through—by the service, the intervention of—Him (the Son) all things should be completely reconciled
back to Himself, whether on earth or in heaven, as through Him [the
Father] made peace by means of the blood of His cross" (Col. 1:20).

Sixth Barricade—Identification

"For just as [because of union of nature] in Adam all people die, so
also [by virtue of their union of nature] shall all in Christ be made
alive" (1 Cor. 15:22).

Every person, when he is born physically, has a position in the first
Adam. This means that man is born with an identification with Adam.
We share Adam's position of spiritual death. Therefore, we are born
sinners. Also, we can't, in our own cunning, change this dead
relationship with Adam.

God erased this barricade by providing a new position which is
identification with Christ. Our new identity means that we are placed
in union with Christ forever. We move into this situation by faith in
Christ as Savior. Once we have been transferred, by the Holy Spirit,
into this new position, we can in no way be removed.

"And He raised us up together with Him and made us sit down together—giving us joint seating with Him—in the heavenly sphere [by virtue of our being] in Christ Jesus, the Messiah, the Anointed One" (Eph. 2:6).

In spite of God's wonderful work of grace-salvation on man's behalf, we remain sinners. However, we now have an alternative to our slavery to sin, a solution to our separation from God, and a second birth which can quicken us to spiritual life. In addition, because of Christ's work on the cross, even though God cannot accept our sin-nature human goodness, he can impute to us his divine goodness (See 2 Cor. 5:21). Therefore, we can become, through faith in Jesus Christ, acceptable to him even though we are sinners.

Since his righteous and just character has been satisfied at the cross, God is now free to express his love to us in terms of his eternal life. God has done what we could not do. He removed the barricades. Yet, God's work was not yet completed. Jesus Christ had to do more than remove the obstructions which Satan had placed between God and mankind. A way had to be provided whereby man of his own free will could choose to allow God to reestablish with him a personal relationship. This brings us to a final step in God's providing salvation grace.

The Barricade Exchange

In the perfect plan of God, once the barricades were banished, an exciting exchange took place. Because Christ came to earth as true humanity and lived a perfect life, he was qualified to remove the barriers. In addition, as a part of God's plan, Jesus could deliberately station himself between righteous God and sinful man.

Thus, the old negative barricades that were against man are eradicated from the mind of God. But a barrier still remains; it is positive and in man's favor. The new barricade is God the Son—Jesus Christ. Now, in the economy of God's grace-glories, what does this divine exchange mean for us? It means the issue clarified, our volition challenged, and God's victory concluded. These axioms become a reality for us when we exchange our *separation* for his *salvation*.

The Issue Clarified

When Jesus Christ went to the cross, all sins were poured out on him and judged. All sins were paid for on the cross. This allowed him to take our place. He placed himself in our position. He set himself up as our substitute. This means that Christ's finished work on the cross has made peace with God available for all.

"And God purposed that through—by the service, the intervention of—Him (the Son) all things should be completely reconciled back to Himself, whether on earth or in heaven, as through Him [the Father] made peace by means of the blood of His cross" (Col. 1:20).

When Jesus placed himself between mankind and God, he clarified the issue once and for all. What is the issue? *What will you do with Jesus?* Consequently, for the unbeliever, the issue in his relationship with God is no longer the barricade of sin. We make a miserable mistake and hinder the salvation ministry of the Holy Spirit when we approach an unbeliever, to introduce him to Jesus, and make the issue sin.

The issue in Grace for Salvation is not sin, *but what Christ did about sin.* It is presented in the message of the gospel—the good news of salvation. "For I am not ashamed of the Gospel (good news) *of Christ;* for it is God's power working unto salvation (for deliverance from eternal death) to every one who believes *with* a personal trust *and* a confident surrender *and* firm reliance, to the Jew first and also to the Greek" (Rom. 1:16). Now we can believe the good news and receive the salvation that solved the sin problem.

Our Volition Challenged

God's purpose in creating mankind was to provide a vehicle for his glory to all his creation. "So that we who first hoped in Christ—who first put our confidence in Him—[have been destined and appointed] to live for the praise of His glory!" (Eph. 1:12). Therefore, it was essential that each person have the capacity to make his own decisions. God made man with a free will.

So, with the cross, God the Father set up an eternal challenge of man's volition. Each person must be confronted with the cross and make a decision about Jesus. Furthermore, God has placed only one restriction upon himself. He will not tamper with man's free will. If any member of the human race perishes, it will be because of his own choice.

There are two areas where our volition comes into play in appropriating *salvation-grace*. First, God-awareness. When an individual reaches the age of accountability, he will either be negative or positive toward God. If he is negative, he has no desire to have a personal relationship with God. Technically then, God has no responsibility to see that he hears the gospel. However, God's love may provide many hearings for him before he leaves the world.

If a person is positive toward God at the time of God awareness, he desires to know more about God and is willing to consider relating personally with him. This does not constitute salvation, but rather, a receptive attitude toward the idea that God is real.

This brings us to the second place our volition is involved when we hear the gospel. When an unbeliever is positive toward God at the time of God-awareness, he is assured of hearing the gospel. At the time of gospel hearing, he will have opportunity to receive Christ as Savior. If he says yes to Christ, he will be forever saved. If he says no, he will remain spiritually lost and separated from God.

A negative response to the gospel by any member of the human race means he remains under the wrath and judgment of God. The church, the body of Christ, is scattered throughout the world to point every unbeliever to Jesus and to warn them of God's impending payday. However, most unbelievers seem more amused by the church's efforts than amazed by the Master's message. Instead of reaching out to receive redemption, they are either indifferent to, or they ridicule their only Redeemer.

Unbelievers evidence intelligence; they are progressive in their concerns of eating and drinking, buying and selling, planting and building. But they are ignorant of God's grace provisions for their deliverance. Yes, the throngs of lost humanity are blindly ignorant to the ill wind of their separation from God. Because unbelievers are cut off from God, they fail to discern what time it is, which way the wind is blowing, and what the score is. They know a lot of things which are not important, but they are unaware of the certainties found in the Bible. They could say yes to Jesus, but they continue to say no.

So, man has two options. He either accepts Christ or rejects him at the time of gospel hearing. Thus, the barricade exchange confronts all people with the challenge: What will you do with Jesus?

God's Victory Concluded

In the mind of God, the sin barriers have been replaced by Jesus Christ. This issue is clarified as the good news. In addition, man's free will is challenged. He must accept or reject Jesus as the Savior. As a third benefit from the barricade exchange, a twofold victory is assured.

First, heaven is assured for the believer. When we leave this world, we will go to be with God forever. God's judgment and second death have been cancelled. We will have a new home. We are assured of an eternal inheritance. In heaven we will not have a sin principle in us to interfere with God's work in our lives. At the rapture, we will receive a spiritual body exactly like Jesus'. Thus, God has many wonderful things for us in heaven. Furthermore, he will make sure we get there to receive all he has prepared. In fact, Jesus is coming again to take us to heaven. "And when (if) I go and make ready a place for you, I will come back again and will take you to Myself, that where I am you may be also" (John 14:3).

Second, during this lifetime every believer has the potential for daily mental stability in every confrontation. God doesn't require us to do the best we can while we live here on earth with only anticipation of blessings in heaven. Rather, we have the *assurance* of heaven now, plus the *reality* of God's presence in us in the person of the Holy Spirit. This means that genuine mental victory can be accomplished in and through us by the Holy Spirit, as we grow in grace-thinking, through learning Bible knowledge.

"But grow in grace (undeserved favor, spiritual strength) and recognition *and* knowledge *and* understanding of our Lord and Savior Jesus Christ, the Messiah. To Him [be] glory (honor, majesty and splendor) both now and to the day of eternity. Amen—so be it!" (2 Pet. 3:18).

This positive mental approach is ours as we acknowledge that God the Holy Spirit is alive in us and consistently take into our minds Bible information. The indwelling Holy Spirit uses this Bible knowledge to provide mental stability, divine guidance, and discernment in each situation we encounter. Also, the Holy Spirit is allowed to teach us God's viewpoint toward our environment. The result will be spiritual common sense and a wholesome sense of humor. Thus, our victory is not only heaven, but every day during this lifetime. We can live undefeated lives and become *more than a conqueror* in the midst of all the circumstances of life.

In the mind of our Maker, because of Christ's work on the cross, every barricade erected by Satan between God and man was erased. Every condition in the perfect character of God which would deny a relationship with man was satisfied. Every flaw of sin in man's soul was paid for and banished. Every brick in the wall of evil was broken down and swept away.

This is God's *Grace for Salvation*, which is the sin solution for mankind. We move into this marvelous relationship by grace through faith in Jesus Christ as Savior.

Summary

1. God the Father, God the Son, God the Holy Spirit are absolutely righteous (Ps. 145:17).
2. Mankind is totally unrighteous (Isa. 64:4–6; Rom. 3:10–12).
3. God cannot fellowship with mankind because of sin's separation (Isa. 59:2).
4. God demands absolute righteousness from mankind (Rom. 3:7).
5. In no way can man in his own efforts satisfy God's just demands (Rom. 3:23).
6. Through the work of Jesus Christ on the cross, God accomplished for mankind what man couldn't do for himself. He removed the barricades of sin (2 Cor. 5:19–21).
7. Therefore, God's absolute righteousness and man's unrighteousness meet at the cross (Rom. 5:8).
8. Now, as a result, man can trust Christ as Savior and the Holy Spirit will appropriate to him salvation and abundant living (John 3:16).

2
The New Birth

In this chapter we investigate the appropriation of God's *Grace for Salvation* to our lives. Because the barricades were banished and the sin problem was solved, salvation can be secured by mankind through personal faith in Jesus Christ as Savior. As we have seen, Adam and Eve lost their battle with Satan and his temptations. But the Second Adam, Jesus Christ, defeated sin, death, hell, and Satan himself. So, we can stop fighting the battle with sin, which Adam lost, and accept the victory over sin, which Christ has won. This means that the right relationship with God which Adam and Eve forfeited can be restored to every person's life by grace through faith.

Yes, we can have victory over sin through God's *Grace for Salvation.* This is possible because the chains which bound us in sin have been blasted away by the blood of Christ. Anyone who remains in sin's slavery does so by his own failure to respond to God through faith. The procedure which God uses to appropriate salvation to our lives is called the new birth. "Jesus answered him, I assure you, most solemnly I tell you, that unless a person is born again (anew, from above), he cannot ever see—know, be acquainted with [and experience]—the kingdom of God" (John 3:3). So it is important that we discuss the basis and the blessings of the new birth.

The Basis

The basis of the new birth is centered in the fact that every aspect of God's grace-provisions was planned in eternity before the world began. We cannot nor are we compelled to work for, earn, or deserve any of God's provisions. In addition, we cannot add anything to what God has provided. This means that God's *Grace for Salvation* was made available before God created man. It is totally the production of God. All that God can do for us is a free gift on the basis of the cross.

Furthermore, all the Trinity—God the Father, God the Son, and God the Holy Spirit—was involved in the plan; and they are now active in its provisions and appropriation to our lives. "Even as [in His love] He chose us—actually picked us out for Himself as His own—in Christ before the foundation of the world" (Eph. 1:4).

In eternity past a grace-conference was held by the Trinity. "God said, let us [Father, Son, and Holy Spirit] make mankind in Our image, after Our likeness" (Gen. 1:26).

At this conference, they decided to make mankind, and to delegate to him domination over all creation. God's purpose in creating mankind was to have a vehicle through which he might be glorified. *Glory* means to picture something in its truest form. Mankind is to be a vehicle and a vital demonstration of God's likeness to all who cross his pathway. "So that we who first hoped in Christ—who first put our confidence in Him—[have been destined and appointed] to live for the praise of His glory!" (Eph. 1:12).

Let's discuss the Trinity's involvement in providing and appropriating God's *Grace for Salvation.*

God the Father Planned Grace for Salvation

In order for mankind to be effective as a vehicle of glory to the Godhead, manifesting its fairness and fullness to all creation, he had to possess a free will. God the Father decided, before he made mankind, to provide him with the volition to choose. In his omniscience, God knew that with a free will man would willfully sin. Before the world began, God made provisions for man's salvation.

God the Father called or elected God the Son to come into time as true humanity to be our Savior. At God the Father's direction, Jesus Christ would come and die on the cross. He would conquer death in order to solve the sin problem. God the Son accepted the election. As a result, in the mind of God, man was saved before he was created. This means that prior to the cross if anyone believed the promise that a Messiah would come, he was saved on the basis of his faith. In post-cross times, we are saved by faith because we believe he has come. Pre-cross people looked forward to the cross. We look back to the cross.

Therefore, God predesigned a plan whereby all who aligned themselves by faith to Jesus Christ as Savior, would share his destiny forever. Those who leave this world rejecting Christ will be cut off from God for all eternity. Their eternal separation will result from their own negative response. God, by no means, made any provision to prevent man from having a right relationship with him. In fact, the opposite is true. God did all that his omnipotence could do to assure mankind that the way to eternal separation was blocked.

Through Jesus' death and resurrection, the way to hell was blocked for mankind. If any human being goes there, he must first remove Christ. This is accomplished through rejecting Jesus as Savior. Hell was not designed for mankind. Rather, it was prepared for the devil and his angels (Matt. 25:41). Man has to choose over God's will to remain cut off from God. God is not willing that any should perish (2 Pet. 3:9).

God the Son Provided Salvation

After the fall from fellowship with God through their folly, Adam and Eve were faced with hang-ups. They were on their own and had to face decisions and work out their problems separated from God's adequacy. Their inconsistencies are amplified in Genesis 3:7–12. Adam and Eve hid from God and evidenced fear of the one who had met every need before their disobedience. Also, they refused to take responsibility for their actions. They blamed God and each other for their ruin. In spite of their negative notions and their neglecting to seek fellowship with God, he came seeking them out by name. This is God's grace in action.

In Genesis 3:15, God demonstrated his grace-intentions when he initiated his plan to restore to mankind the relationship which Adam had recklessly ruined. "And I will put enmity between you and the woman, and between your offspring and her offspring; He shall bruise *and* tread your head under foot and you will lie in wait *and* bruise His heel" (Gen. 3:15). This means that God's plan of salvation-grace is to be provided through the natural birth process by the power of the Holy Spirit. Even though Jesus accepted his election to come and execute salvation, he could not do so as God. Being coequal and coeternal with God the Father and God the Holy Spirit, he is sovereignty and eternal life. Sovereignty and eternal life cannot die. So, God the Son had to become a man and live in true humanity. He would have a free will minus an anti-God sin nature.

Then, God established the Hebrew nation to be the messengers and the custodians of the messianic promise. They were to be the vehicles to perpetuate the promise of the coming Messiah. Thus, the Old Testament is an account of how Satan sought to hinder and to prevent God's perfect plan of salvation. With a multitude of maneuvers, Satan constantly attempted to sever the messianic line in order to prevent Jesus Christ's birth.

But, Satan failed, and Jesus was born in the manger in Bethlehem of the virgin Mary. He lived on earth as perfect humanity, with a free will, minus a sin nature or any personal sins. He could have sinned, but he did not. Remember, we don't commit sins because we have a sin nature. *We sin because we have a free will.* Adam didn't have a sin nature, but he had a free will and chose to sin. Jesus, the Second Adam, was also minus a sin nature. He had a free will but chose not to sin.

Therefore, Jesus ascended the cross as a perfect sacrifice for sin. He was fully God and fully man. But he lived here on earth in the role of perfect humanity. Because he didn't sin, he was qualified to be our sin-bearer and to pay for the sins of every person—past, present, and future. He secured our salvation as he died on the cross spiritually and arose from the dead. Spiritual death means to be separated or cut off from God.

"He personally bore our sins in His [own] body to the tree [as to an altar and offered Himself on it] that we might die (cease to exist) to sin and live to righteousness. By His wounds you have been healed" (1 Pet. 2:24).

Remember, it was the perfect humanity of Jesus Christ separated from God the Father and God the Holy Spirit which secured our salvation. Then, he said, "It is finished." No one killed the physical life of Jesus. The wounds inflicted certainly played a part. But Jesus gave up his physical life of his own volition. He did so after he had finished his work of being judged for our sin. "And Jesus, crying out with a loud voice, said, Father, into Your hands I commit My spirit! And with these words He expired" (Luke 23:46).

God the Holy Spirit Perpetuates Salvation

God the Father planned our salvation. God the Son provided it. God the Holy Spirit perpetuates it when any person trusts Jesus

Christ as Savior. This is accomplished because when Jesus ascended to heaven, he kept a promise made to the disciples in the upper room. He sent the Holy Spirit to indwell every believer. This occurred at Pentecost. The Holy Spirit is the Comforter who reveals the revolutionary truths about God the Father. He convicts the unbeliever of sin through the witnessing of the believer. He uses the believer to teach the unbeliever about the cross and the availability of God's *Grace for Salvation*. He reveals to the world that faith in Christ is the only possible deliverance for mankind from God's judgment.

He is the power of God in the world restraining the forces of evil fostered by Satan and his soldiers. The moment a person believes in Christ as Savior, the Holy Spirit indwells him and will never leave or forsake him (Heb. 13:5–6). His major ministry to believing mankind is to use Bible truth in order to provide mental stability in all situations. Furthermore, he uses Bible knowledge stored in our minds to teach us God's viewpoint toward life and to touch the lives of others through our yielded behavior.

The basis for God's *Grace for Salvation* is the Godhead. The entire plan, procedure, and provisions of salvation depend totally upon God. Also, the appropriation and perpetuation of *Grace for Salvation* depend entirely on him and never on anything mankind can do.

The Blessing

Since the new birth is based on God's character and is his work, what is man's responsibility? It is the response of faith. Faith is not a work which man accomplishes. Initiatively, it is the nonmeritorious attitude of belief in the gospel message. This allows the Holy Spirit to give us the incentive to receive Jesus as Savior. Because we believed the gospel and acknowledged Jesus as Savior, the Holy Spirit moved into our lives and performed the new birth. Furthermore, God takes the initiative through the convicting ministry of the Holy Spirit and the use of Bible knowledge to lead us to exercise our faith in him throughout our lifetime.

With Bible knowledge in our minds, the Holy Spirit can motivate us to pray, to worship, and to want more Bible knowledge. He can teach us the Father's viewpoint and steady us as each situation arises. Therefore, we can't even take credit for believing in Christ as Savior or living by faith after salvation. "Looking away [from all that will distract] to Jesus, Who is the Leader *and* the Source of *our* faith [giving the first incentive for our belief] and is also its Finisher [bringing it to maturity and perfection]" (Heb. 12:2).

The blessings of the new birth can be summarized as a twofold victory.

First, we have victory over life and death for all eternity. Heaven is assured. Once we are born again, we need no longer concern ourselves with our destination after physical death. We will go to be with God forever.

Second, we have the potential of daily victory amid every routine, responsibility, and relationship. It is this daily victory that many believers fail to enjoy. We have God's wonderful eternal security. We can face no condemnation because we are positioned forever in Jesus Christ. We share his life.

However, many Christians fail to realize and enjoy most of the grace-provisions which God the Father has made available for them experientially in this lifetime.

So many believers depend on anything and everything but God, unaware that every breath they breathe and every moment they live is a result of God's grace-provisions. They seem to think that they have all they need to be all they should be, but apart from God's personal influence. To claim that we can be independent and self-sufficient without God is a dangerous attitude. Such an attitude can cause us to believe that we can avoid God and lose nothing.

Some claim to be a man's man or self-made. They are proud that no one could call them weak. They convince themselves that to claim a need for God in daily living is to use a weakling's crutch. With this attitude, they will never have time for God. Their lives will be centered around what they think will make them self-sufficient and independent. They will operate on the premise that God can do nothing for them in coping with life in the raw. They will refuse to admit that they need anything from God, except salvation. They will reject the concepts of grace and convince themselves that God is irrelevant to the business of living and the fun of life.

This carnal attitude can give us a false sense of self-importance. We can become so impressed with ourselves and our own ability that God can do nothing for us. We will give lip service to the presence of God but see no personal relevance in relying on God's power moment by moment. We may consider our relationship with God as subjective thinking and pride ourselves on being practical persons of action. This carnal thinking hinders our experiencing the daily victory God has provided.

How can this twofold victory be applied to our lives? The answer is the ministry of the Holy Spirit. The moment we trusted Jesus as Savior, the Holy Spirit appropriated to our lives at least six spiritual principles.

The Holy Spirit Performed the New Birth

We were born again. We became spiritually alive. This means that we can understand spiritual phenomenon. We can relate personally to God the Father through Jesus. We can also store up Bible promises and Bible knowledge. As a result, the basic principles of the Bible begin to make sense. We begin to take more interest in what the Bible teaches about the areas of life in which we are involved. "Who owe their birth neither to bloods, nor to the will of the flesh [that of physical impulse], nor to the will of man [that of a father], but to God.—They are born of God!" (John 1:13).

We Were Baptized with the Holy Spirit

This means that at the time of our salvation experience, the Holy Spirit placed us in union with Christ forever. We were identified with Christ. This is our eternal security. It can never be changed. "For by (means of the personal agency of) one (Holy) Spirit we were all, whether Jews or Greeks, slaves or free, baptized [and by baptism united together] into one body, and all made to drink of one (Holy) Spirit" (1 Cor. 12:13).

We Were Indwelt with the Holy Spirit

The concept here is that the Holy Spirit moved into our minds and took up permanent residence in our lives. In addition, we have the assurance that he will never leave us or forsake us (Heb. 13:5–6). "Do you know that your body is the temple—the very sanctuary—of the Holy Spirit Who lives within you, Whom you have received [as a Gift] from God? You are not your own" (1 Cor. 6:19).

At the Moment of Salvation, We Were Sealed by the Holy Spirit

When we were saved by grace through faith, God stamped us with the seal of the Holy Spirit. The Holy Spirit's presence within our minds is God's guarantee that we shall receive the inheritance he has waiting for us. The fact that the Holy Spirit is alive in us is God's pledge or down payment that we will someday be with God forever. Furthermore, his presence provides a foretaste now of what heaven will be like. So, we can praise God continually, if we know and believe his Word. "That [Spirit] is the guarantee of our inheritance— the first fruit, the pledge and foretaste, the down payment of our heritage" (Eph. 1:14).

We Were Given at Least One Spiritual Gift

We must distinguish between the gift which is the Holy Spirit, and the gifts of the Holy Spirit. Every believer has the Gift from the moment of his salvation experience. However, the gifts of the Holy Spirit are bestowed by him as he wills at the moment of salvation. The gifts are not for the believer's personal gratification but for the normal and healthy functioning of the church—the body of Christ.

Also, the gifts which we received at our new birth are not what we can do for God, but what he can do in and through our lives as we relax into his control. The gifts of the Holy Spirit are not necessarily our talents. However, our natural abilities may be used in the operation of our gifts. The gifts are not universally bestowed. This means that no one is given all the gifts, nor does the Holy Spirit give to every believer any one of the gifts. For example, God doesn't call every believer to be a pastor or an evangelist.

In addition, we are not to seek the gifts of the Spirit. The Holy Spirit cannot be coerced into giving the gifts we desire. He gives them as he wills at the moment of salvation. Instead, we are to seek the more excellent way, love. Even this right mental attitude, love, is produced by the Holy Spirit as we live under his control (Rom. 5:5). Also, we are not to make an issue of the gifts lest we cause confusion, imitate the unbeliever, and take credit for what is accomplished in our lives by the Holy Spirit. Our responsibility is to relax into the Holy Spirit. Our responsibility is to relax into the Holy Spirit's control moment by moment and situation by situation in order for the Holy Spirit to exercise his gifts through our routines, responsibilities, and relationships.

WARNING! Emotional feelings and dramatic experiences can be a result of the functioning of the gifts of the Holy Spirit in our lives, but not necessarily a manifestation of them (1 Cor. 12:8–13).

We Were Given Eternal Security

"And I give them eternal life, and they shall never lose it *or* perish throughout the ages—to all eternity they shall never by any means be destroyed. And no one is able to snatch them out of My hand" (John 10:28).

There can be no positive, victorious Christian life apart from a firm handle on eternal security. Why can we believe that once we are saved, we cannot lose our salvation? The answer stands out in the Scriptures as a mandate of God's mercy. At the moment we trusted Christ as Savior, God the Holy Spirit established for us an eternal, unchangeable relationship with God the Father. Heaven is thus assured for the believer. Once we move into the plan of God, we can never get out. There is no sin that can remove us from God's *Grace for Salvation*. This is not a license to sin; rather it is freedom to live and relate to God as a vehicle of his love.

Many believers are confused with the false concept that at the moment of salvation, they, of their own free will, placed themselves *into* God's *Grace for Salvation*. Therefore, they claim that they can take themselves *out* of his plan. This is a sin-nature philosophical principle which has no sound scriptural support. In reality, we do not put ourselves into God's plan. Rather, we believe the gospel through the nonmeritorious response of faith, and the Holy Spirit places us in union with Christ forever. He does the work. This attitude of faith is not a work on our part nor does it obligate God. Instead it allows God the Holy Spirit to appropriate salvation to our lives. The work of salvation is totally the work of God, so we cannot take ourselves out of his plan.

We can believe in eternal security because it is logical and consistent with the character of God. It depends totally on whom and what God is and not on our feelings and experiences. At the moment of salvation, God gets hold on us. We do not hold onto him. Instead, we hold onto Bible doctrines, and we claim Bible promises, and he will never let go of us. Also, we can believe in eternal security because God is sovereign. He doesn't undo what he designs. "If we are faithless (do not believe and are untrue to Him), He remains true [faithful to His Word and His righteous character], for He cannot deny Himself" (2 Tim. 2:13).

God wills that the Christian life begin with the new birth. Birth cannot be undone. In addition, God is immutable. He doesn't change his mind about us. We can trust in his faithfulness. "I know that whatever God does, it endures for ever; nothing can be added to it, nor anything taken from it; and God does it so that men will (reverently) fear Him—know that He is, revere and worship Him" (Eccl. 3:14).

The tenses of the Greek language also teach eternal security. For example, in Acts 16:31 we read, "Believe on the Lord Jesus Christ, and thou shalt be saved" (KJV). The word for "saved" is in the aorist tense. The idea conveyed is that in a moment of time we believe in Jesus Christ for salvation. At that moment it is appropriated to our lives, through the ministry of the Holy Spirit. Immediately the work and the results are divorced from time. This means that nothing in time can change it. Furthermore, the process of salvation is perpetuated forever. This happens because God's *Grace for Salvation* is not only his work, but it is sealed by the Holy Spirit.

God's sealing indicates his ownership and his guarantee of salvation. From the moment the Holy Spirit moved into our lives, we have belonged to God and nothing can change it. God's sealing also implies his protection under a permanent contract. Once we believe in him as Savior, God the Holy Spirit establishes a contract. God's signature is the indwelling Holy Spirit made possible through the work of the cross. Our signature is the response of nonmeritorious faith in the gospel message that he is the Savior. Eternal security is not wishful thinking. Jesus Christ is qualified and able to present us faultless to the Father after physical death.

"Now to Him Who is able to keep you without stumbling, *or* slipping, *or* falling and to present [you] unblemished (blameless and faultless) before the presence of His glory—with unspeakable, ecstatic delight—in triumphant joy *and* exultation" (Jude 24).

The new birth is God's grace-provision for salvation. Once we are born again, we have a living hope based on the resurrection of Jesus Christ. Because he was raised from the dead, we have the assurance that our eternal inheritance is beyond destruction. God himself is preserving it for us. He is also taking care of us here, and he will make sure we get to heaven to enjoy it. This means that we can experience God's stability and peace of mind during this lifetime even though we may experience manifold pressures, adversities, trials, and temptations (1 Pet. 1:4–6).

The grace-approach to salvation means that God does the work, mankind can be benefited by God's work through faith, and God receives the credit. In the religious and legalistic approach to salvation and the Christian life, man does the work for God, God is supposed to be blessed by what man does, and man receives the credit. Christianity is not a religion. It is a relationship with God which is established, maintained, and sustained by God. Thus, salvation is God's free gift to mankind.

In summary, the key which unlocks this aspect of God's garden of grace is our personal faith in Jesus Christ as Savior. Our positive response to the gospel allowed the Holy Spirit to appropriate God's *Grace for Salvation* to our lives. He performed the new birth. As we leave this area, we can rejoice every day in the fact of our salvation. Regardless of any contrary confrontations, we can always know and be thankful that we are saved for all eternity. We have a basic reason to celebrate out relationship with God. He has done for us that which we could never do for ourselves.

We can also rejoice because God's *Grace for Salvation* sets the stage for abundant living. Therefore, every day can be an exciting adventure because we know the reality of being born again and the comfort of the Holy Spirit's control.

Summary

1. God has provided *Grace for Salvation* for every person. God the Father planned it; God the Son came in true humanity and executed the plan on the cross.
2. Salvation-Grace must be appropriated. God the Holy Spirit relates it to our lives the moment we believe the gospel and change our minds about God.
3. First, we become aware of God at the age of accountability. If we

are positive toward God, he will make sure we hear the gospel. God-awareness doesn't constitute salvation. There must be a faith response to the gospel.

4. Then, we hear the gospel. Because we are positive toward God at the time of gospel hearing, we believe the gospel. This non-meritorious response of faith is our repentance. As we believe the gospel, we change our minds toward God.

5. Next, the Holy Spirit moves into our lives and appropriates Salvation-Grace in terms of the new birth.

6. Thus, we have an eternal future based totally on the work of God and his perfect essence.

7. In addition, we have the fantastic potential of abundant, positive, victorious living in every routine, reponsibility, and relationship.

Part II
Grace for Living

Our first stop in God's garden of grace-provisions was *Grace for Salvation.* In this area, we discovered that God has provided all we need to be saved from sin and eternal separation from him. Now, we move to the second area which I call *Grace for Living.* This concept of God's grace includes all that God has provided to keep us alive in a world of anti-God thinking. In this division I deal with *"Provisions for Daily Living"* and *"Dependent Availability."*

3
Provisions for Daily Living

At the moment of salvation, we were placed into a twofold spiritual position.

First, we were positioned "in Christ." This is our eternal, permanent relationship with God. We are new creations. We sit in a heavenly place spiritually in Christ. "And He raised us up together with Him and made us sit down together—giving us joint seating with Him—in the heavenly sphere [by virtue of our being] in Christ Jesus, the Messiah, the Anointed One" (Eph. 2:6).

Second, we have the very presence of Christ in us. He was positioned in us at the moment of salvation. We share his divine nature and his eternal life in the person of the Holy Spirit. This second spiritual condition is our daily fellowship with God. "Do you know that your body is the temple—the very sanctuary—of the Holy Spirit Who lives within you, Whom you have received [as a Gift] from God? You are not your own" (1 Cor. 6:19).

The implications of "in Christ Jesus" relate to our eternal destination and the assurance of heaven. But God has done more than assure us of heaven some day. In the provisions of *Grace for Salvation*, God did not say, "You have trusted me for salvation; therefore, heaven is assured. One day you will be with me forever. At that time, I will begin to bless you continually. In the meantime, as you live out your days on earth, just do the best you can in coping with life and in being my witnesses. When things are rough, just remember that you are saved and some day you will be victorious."

Now it is true that we are saved forever at the moment of salvation and that one day we will go to heaven. But "Christ in you" is also a fantastic provision of God's grace package. Its implications relate to blessings now on a daily basis. In God's *Grace-for-Living* provisions he says to us: "You have trusted me for salvation; therefore heaven is assured. However, I am not leaving you alone in the world. I have sent the Holy Spirit to indwell you from the moment of salvation. I have placed my living Word in you. Through the Spirit's control, as you feed on my written Word, you can enjoy mental stability, live with a positive attitude, and experience victory in every confrontation."

So, our salvation experience is only the beginning. Within God's grace package is contained all that we need for survival and positive living every day. As we explore this area of *Grace for Living*, we shall begin to comprehend some of God's marvelous provisions for daily living.

The Grace-for-Living Package

The concept of *Grace for Living* refers to all the many details of life which are available to every believer through Christ Jesus. For example, the air we breathe and the natural laws which govern the universe are God's grace provisions. In addition, *Grace for Living* includes such things as material blessings, money, cars, lands, houses, and food. Then there are many supplies for emotional and mental needs such as loved ones, sex, pleasure, status symbols, friends, and social provisions. The truth that must be recognized is that all the details of life are the grace provisions of God. This means that God has made available all that we need for the kind of living he has designed for us here.

"His divine power has bestowed upon us all things that [are requisite and suited] to life and godliness, through the (full, personal) knowledge of Him Who called us by *and* to His own glory and excellence (virtue)" (2 Pet. 1:3).

In *Grace for Salvation*, our volition is involved. Each person must make a decision for or against Jesus Christ. But in *Grace for Living* our volition is not involved. God provides the details of life. They are ours. We cannot do a thing to provide them for ourselves. Our mental attitudes determine that we may or may not enjoy them properly and use them wisely, but our volition is not involved in their availability. "My God will liberally supply (fill to the full) your every need according to His riches in glory in Christ Jesus" (Phil. 4:19).

The details-of-life package is a vital part of every one's life. We are surrounded by things from the moment we are born. So, it's essential that we learn to relate to them on the basis of grace. Otherwise, they can become more important to us than God. In fact, some of them could become gods in our thinking. So often we hear of certain heathen cultures worshiping idols. But in reality, we may have more "strange gods" here in America than any other place on earth. Some people refer to America as a "Christian" nation. We are grateful to God for our fantastic advantages. Actually, true Christianity, free of idols, is in the minority in our land.

We operate by a strange philosophy in which we are willing to send missionaries into a foreign land to preach the gospel truths which many believers refuse to practice here. When adhered to, God's Word can cause commotion in any culture. It can divide homes and bring ostracism. It can cause suffering and even death. We seem to have no reluctance to dump such a powerful idea as the Gospel into a foreign culture, yet refuse to allow it to interfere with our idols here at home. Many hold the gospel with one hand and fondle their idols with the other.

This is not the fault of the gospel, but our idolatry can destroy its effectiveness. An idol is something or someone we have come to love more than God. God never intended for his provisions to become more important to us than our position to him.

Paul tells us in 1 Corinthians 10:14 to flee idolatry. To flee a detail that has become an idol, we must change our mind about it and as a result, it will be used for the purpose for which it was created. If we are to love God as we ought, we must not worship any of the details of life. We live in a world which is dominated by anti-God thinking. In addition, we all have a sin nature. We can become too attached to things.

When we set up in our minds some detail of life as an idol, we are paying allegiance to Satan, and we are disobeying God's command not to love the world. So many believers allow their liberty to become license. They seek to appease the natural appetites of their anti-God nature and avoid any teachings which would conflict with their enjoyments. At the same time, they try to claim Jesus as Lord.

We need to relate to the details of life, but we must not allow our lives to become occupied with them. The only safeguard against any detail becoming an idol is to be occupied by Jesus Christ in the person of the Holy Spirit, moment by moment and situation by situation.

Only as we relate properly to God can we have the proper grace-relationship to God's *Grace-for-Living* package. From this grace-approach, we can be that colony of heaven on earth whose conduct will befit our true citizenship.

The Grace-for-Living Perspective

The proper perspective toward the details of *Grace for Living* is found in our mental attitude. God created the human mind and holds the handle for its proper function. Our minds are an open book to him. He allows us freedom of thought and freedom of choice. Yet we are responsible for our thoughts as well as our choices. Even though we are often judged on the basis of our behavior, our actions are determined, motivated, and influenced by what goes on in our minds. Life is lived in our thinking. "For as he thinks in his heart, so is he. As one who reckons he says to you, eat and drink, yet his heart is not with you [but is grudging the cost]" (Prov. 23:7).

Our approach to life, the effectiveness of our behavior, our physical attractiveness, and even our health are greatly dependent upon what we think. Furthermore, our thought processes are determined by the quality of information which we allow to dominate our thinking. So, there are two specific areas of knowledge which are vital to our lives.

First, there is the vast host of secular knowledge which enables us to make a living, relate to our environment, and understand physical phenomenon.

Second, we have available the written Word of God which is even more important than the knowledge of the world. Through God's knowledge, we are able to relate to spiritual phenomenon and to build a life acceptable and pleasing to God.

Each of these bodies of information will produce in our thinking its own specific mental approaches to life. Now, there are many different mental attitudes but only two basic viewpoints towards life.

First, there is man's viewpoint based on secular information under the sin nature's control.

Second, there is God's viewpoint based on Bible knowledge under the Holy Spirit's control.

These two perspectives are the sources of a constant struggle in every believer's life.

As believers, we are not of the world, but we are in the world. This means that the norms and standards and the world's philosophies constantly bombard us from all angles. The world of anti-God thinking pressures the believer to conform to human standards.

"See to it that no one carries you off as spoil *or* makes you yourselves captive by his so-called philosophy *and* intellectualism, and vain deceit (idle fancies and plain nonsense), following human tradition—men's ideas of the material [rather than the spiritual] world—just crude notions following the rudimentary *and* elemental teachings of the universe, and disregarding [the teachings of] Christ, the Messiah" (Col. 2:8).

God the Father desires for us to be transformed in our thinking based on his norms and standards. "Do not be conformed to this world—this age, fashioned after and adapted to its external, superficial customs. But be transformed (changed) by the [entire] renewal of your mind—by its new ideals and its new attitude—so that you may prove [for yourselves] what is the good and acceptable and perfect will of God, *even* the thing which is good and acceptable and perfect [in His sight for you]" (Rom. 12:2).

We have the possibility of two basic perspectives toward the provisions of *Grace for Living*—human perspective and divine perspective. Let's examine both of these viewpoints in relationship to the details of life.

The Human Perspective

Human-viewpoint thinking originated with Satan when he revolted against God in eternity past.

"You said in your heart, I will ascend to Heaven; I will exalt my throne above the stars of God; I will sit upon the mount of assembly in the uttermost north;

"I will ascend above the heights of the clouds, I will make myself like the Most High" (Isa. 14:13–14). It was launched into the human race through Adam's fall. "When the woman saw that the tree was good (suitable and pleasant) for food, and that it was delightful to look at and a tree to be desired to make one wise, she took of its fruit and ate; and she gave some also to her husband, and he ate" (Gen. 3:6).

In no way can Satan indwell the believer. So, he centers his attack on God through our minds. He will use every factor that influences our minds to neutralize us and to make us casualties in God's army against evil. Satan will use our environment, our background, our training, our culture, or anything which conditions our thinking to encourage us to function apart from God's control. Even though he cannot possess us, in this way he can infiltrate our thinking with his negative viewpoint toward God. When we adopt Satan's anti-God viewpoint, it becomes our human perspective.

The basic treatise of human perspective is that we can be as smart as God. We can, by our own efforts, solve the world's problems as well as our own and establish a perfect environment on earth. Human viewpoint says that successful living consists of the abundance of things, and that we must do all that is necessary to get them. The smarter we are, and the harder we work, the more we have.

We will tend to be successful believers by means of taboos, ecstatics, and/or asceticism. At the same time, we will consider successful living in terms of physical security and human perspective. Satan's panaceas will sound so beautiful and broadminded. The world's pleasurable and materially profitable life-style will become most attractive. There will be little thought given to pleasing God, even though we are believers. God's way of faith and grace orientation may present a threat to our human endeavors.

From this self-life human viewpoint, we may have good experience and master many situations, but we will never master ourselves. We will profess to be what we are not and invariably something will happen to betray us. The worst thing about using the details of life from the human-viewpoint perspective is that they will find us out. They will show us up at some awkward moment. No matter how hard we may insist on keeping that which God has told us to exterminate, somewhere in our disobedient thinking, we will stand accused by those very things.

In human-viewpoint thinking, there will be times when we are off guard. We will be forced to argue our case, to try to explain, or to justify ourselves. We may give up some worldly amusements, give our goods to feed the poor, or give to God some of our time and talents, but refuse to give ourselves.

Another fatal result of the human perspective is stubbornness. When we attempt to live our lives apart from Bible principles and the control of the Holy Spirit, there will be a lot of inner rebellion hidden under our external religion. Stubbornness can begin early in life, as a child grows up in the home when he is allowed to evidence a disobedient attitude. Stubbornness can break our hearts, wreck our homes, divide our churches, fill our hospital beds and suicide graves. The reason for it all is "self" on the throne of our lives.

Perhaps one of the saddest places to evidence human-viewpoint thinking is in the church fellowship. There are so many believers in our churches who have never surrendered unconditionally to God's will. They lug their sins around with unbroken wills and hard hearts. They pretend to serve God, but in reality, they manifest the old-Adam-nature-parade under the auspices of religion and legalism. Most church fellowships humor this human-viewpoint perspective. They fail to demand Bible repentance. Thus, they can increase their membership with unbelievers who are stiff-necked and proud, pious in their own eyes, yet, not washed of their filthiness. They may gaily accept Christ, but afterwards show little evidence of a new life in Christ.

In this human-perspective approach to the Christian life, we can be unmatched with moral integrity, indicate a selfless sense of duty, and express a tireless concern for the lost. We may demonstrate nobility of character, profess humble dedication, and cap it all off with high and holy ambitions. Yet, we will live in miserable disappointment. We fail to enter God's mental rest and we may become sick of all that reminds us of Christianity.

Basically, human-viewpoint thinking places the emphasis on the outward appearance of things and circumstances. We will tend to emphasize our *status* in life as more important than our *station* in Christ. We will yield to the temptation to evaluate others on the basis of human dynamics such as personality and physical appearance.

From the human perspective, we may measure our success on a comparative basis with those whom we feel are weaker than ourselves. We may even use their weaknesses to inflate our own egos. We may also use the details of *Grace for Living* to escape a "jam" at the expense of others. Our number one priority will be personal survival regardless of the implications.

In addition, we may consider the abundance of things as a measurement of God's favor and approval. Under the influence of such ungodly thinking, we can give lip service to biblical principles and superficial allegiance to our professed faith. However, our life-styles and our attitudes will evidence that our primary concerns center around the abundance of the things we can possess. The result will be that we are mastered by the details of life. We will tend to worship them and will feel compelled to attain them at any cost to ourselves and others.

The paradox is that we will fail to enjoy what we have because we are seeking from them a happiness which they are unable to provide. The details of life were designed to meet our basic human needs and not to provide the mental stability and peace of mind needed to cope with life successfully. The unhappiest people in the world are not always unbelievers. Many times, they are believers who have become entangled in the abundance of things and the cares of the world. They have not learned the secret of God's mental rest, peace of mind, and stability.

Therefore, they reach out for happiness in the things of life as they function in their different routines, responsibilities, and relationships. Again, they do not fully enjoy their activities, or the things they possess beyond mere anticipation of them.

God plans for the believer to be mentally stable regardless of the nature of his situation or circumstances. But when we are not operating on Bible principles under the Holy Spirit's control, hardness of heart or spiritual darkness may develop in our thinking. Thus, we may become frustrated and plagued with inner misery by the very details of life that are meant to be grace-provisions. In order to compensate for our confusion, we may double our efforts on a frantic search for happiness in the things we possess or think we deserve. However, we will not be satisfied.

When we become involved in this covetous attitude toward things, certain dangerous reactions can occur. They will serve only to perpetuate our misery. Such factors as instability, boredom, restlessness, and disillusionment may be present. These are negative mental attitudes which are completely foreign to God's purpose for our lives. Therefore, because of our spiritual darkness, we are miserable with or without the abundance of things. Even though we are denied certain details of life, if the desire for them controls our thinking, we are still slaves to them.

In human-viewpoint thinking, we are always out of focus mentally. We may place our focus on self and what we can accumulate and accomplish on our own. This is an improper objective because our self-life can't be permanently satisfied. The result is frustration. We may focus on people for our happiness. But all people have a sin nature. They fail to provide the stability we need just as we have a sin nature and fail them. Thus, we are disillusioned.

Whether it be self, people, or things, they are sad objectives for happiness. God doesn't compel us to live with such attitudes controlling our thinking. Instead, he demands that we be happy, and God doesn't make a demand without providing a plan and a procedure by which it can be realized.

Thus, we have the option of approaching the details of *Grace for Living* from our own human perspective, separating them from God and relating to them in our own strength alone.

God's Divine Perspective

Grace for Living reveals God's wonderful sense of humor. As believers, we live in the enemy camp—the devil's world. This is the world of anti-God thinking. Yet, the believer is saved forever, and can experience great happiness and victory in the midst of all that Satan can throw against him. The victory, peace of mind, mental stability, and confidence which the believer can have in the world is an embarrassment to Satan. His plan is for man to be self-sufficient, to solve his own problems, and to build a perfect environment apart from God's control. However, our sin nature frustrates Satan's strategy and reduces it to an impossible task.

Thus, in the midst of all the pressures and crises of life, we can be undefeatable and more than a conqueror, as we learn how to relax into the Holy Spirit's control. God has provided all the details of life for our benefit. Therefore, we can only recognize them as such, as we acquire divine viewpoint.

We have the indwelling Holy Spirit. With Bible knowledge in our minds, he can teach God's viewpoint toward every detail of life. "Who has known *or* understood the mind (the counsels and purposes) of the Lord so as to guide *and* instruct [Him] *and* give Him knowledge? But we have the mind of Christ, the Messiah, *and* do hold the thoughts (feelings and purposes) of His heart" (1 Cor. 2:16).

This is the proper perspective and the right relationship toward them. God's viewpoint means that we orient properly to *Grace for*

Living. We live and think with the awareness that the purpose of the details of life is to meet our needs for survival in this world.

We can understand that the details of life were not designed to be worshiped. We can refuse to become a slave to them. From the divine perspective, we are stabilized and the Holy Spirit can sustain us in times of crisis. We realize it is dangerous to consider the things we can possess to be our source of happiness. The details of life come and go. We can easily lose them. In contrast, God's presence and stability are permanent.

Human stability depends on the acquisition of an abundance of things and pleasant circumstances. This places great limitations and strain on enjoying life because so many of our circumstances are not pleasant. Also, much that we possess becomes a burden and may even make us unhappy.

But, God has designed his own stability and happiness for us in eternity past. This means that true happiness is older than the human race, totally dependent on God and cannot be added to by man. God the Father, God the Son, and God the Holy Spirit have always been happy.

Thus, in summary, the proper perspective toward *Grace for Living* is the realization that the details of life were designed to meet our needs for survival in this lifetime. They were not made to provide the inner happiness and the mental stability which we need for successfully coping with the pressures of life. God alone is our source of mental happiness. As we live under the Holy Spirit's control, God will use material things as well as other aspects of the details of life to be avenues of his happiness. But we must not expect God's happiness, if we consider any of the details of life as more important to us than God. Every facet of our lives and all the details of life are provisions from him. Thus, we must acknowledge this and use them as reasons to celebrate our relationship with God.

The Grace-for-Living Payoff

From the divine perspective toward the details of life, comes our proper relationship to *Grace for Living.* Instead of being controlled by the details of life, we are able to master them as Christ is allowed to master our thinking. In this manner, we are able to receive from the details of life the blessings they are designed to give.

There is great victory in operating on the basis of God's divine viewpoint toward *Grace for Living*. We will become tough in our minds. We can refuse to faint and fall apart in the face of adversity. We have a special kind of discernment and a delightful sense of humor. We can laugh at ourselves. We can be relaxed about tomorrow. We will evidence a spiritual common sense which faces life one day at a time. God will be able to use us to influence others not to give up on God or surrender their principles.

We may be physically exhausted and completely defeated from the standpoint of the human odds. But we can still think the things which will allow God to overcome the pressures and adversities of our situations. We think at all times. Therefore, when our thinking is dominated by God's divine perspective, based on Bible knowledge, we are able to discern the real issues of life. God can keep us in proper focus about ourselves and the pressures of life. Thus, to view life from God's perspective and outlook is one of the greatest stabilizers which we have in this lifetime. When we consistently live in God's Word and operate on its principles, we can learn to think soundly, and we will not revert to emotionalism from the human perspective as a substitute for faith-living.

The Bible is God's accurate discerner of what we think. It is his source for straightening out our mental attitude. It's God's umpire for our thinking. It is our most constructive critic. "The Word that God speaks is alive and full of power—making it active, operative, energizing and effective; it is sharper than any two-edge sword, penetrating to the dividing line of the breath of life (soul) and [the immortal] spirit, and of joints and marrow [that is, of the deepest parts of our nature] exposing *and* sifting *and* analyzing *and* judging the very thoughts and purposes of the heart" (Heb. 4:12).

As our thinking becomes consistent with the Word of God, he will have a great impact on those who cross our pathway. As a result, we will experience the by-product of his stability, inner happiness, peace of mind, and the inner strength which cannot be disturbed by problems or prosperity. Worldly, anti-God thinking can be defeated and God's kind of love, a right mental attitude, will dominate our behavior. Therefore, we can survive in the devil's world as living demonstrations of God's availability and adequacy for every confrontation.

When we are occupied with the abundance of things, they can become more important to us than God. We may consider them the only things in life worthwhile. We will misuse them, and they will become a major source of confusion rather than an avenue of God's strength. As a result, if certain things are not available, we will be unhappy. Also, if we accumulate a few things, their luster will soon fade and we are still unhappy. Thus, it is imperative that we master the details of God's *Grace for Living.*

How can this be accomplished? The answer is found in allowing the Holy Spirit to control our thinking and the building of our lives on Bible knowledge and principles. Then, we can be satisfied with or without the details of life. They will be a blessing. Furthermore, if we lose them, we are still stabilized because we are operating on Bible knowledge under the Holy Spirit's control. Therefore, we can enjoy our money, our houses and lands, and our loved ones from the divine viewpoint.

To understand the value of this proper grace-perspective, let us contrast the human viewpoint and the divine viewpoint. We will deal with the detail of food. However, this principle applies to each detail of life which we possess.

First, the human-viewpoint approach. Here our attitude toward physical nourishment would be, "I have the job. I do the work. I make the money. I buy the groceries. I bring them home. I cook the food. I place the food on the table. I eat it. Therefore, I am the one who is providing the needed physical nourishment." I may give God the credit for the strength, but I'm doing it. Now, in this approach the detail of food still meets my hunger need. However, it can do no more because my attitude is wrong. I am not operating on the Bible principle of grace, under the control of the Holy Spirit. Any gratitude to God will be superficial and meaningless.

Second, the divine-perspective approach. From this viewpoint, we are operating from grace-orientation. We are functioning on Bible principles under the Holy Spirit's control. Consequently, our attitude to God will be one of celebration. We will thank God for his presence in us. We will thank him for the job, the health to work and those with whom we work. We will recognize that the food, the grocery store, and the personnel are all part of God's grace-provisions. We will also know that it is God's sufficiency and grace which gives us the strength, the insight and the capability to prepare the food and consume it. Our entire viewpoint will be one of praise to God on the basis of his providing the needed physical nourishment.

Now, with this positive, grace-oriented attitude, we can express genuine appreciation to God for food. Also, in this approach our hunger need is met just as in the human viewpoint approach. However, there are two additional blessings. First, God the Holy Spirit is released in our mental attitude. Therefore, not only is our hunger need met, but we will gratefully use the detail of food as a reason to celebrate our relationship with God. Then, even more fantastic is the fact that because of our understanding of grace, God can use the detail of food as a means to relate to us his peace of mind, inner happiness and confidence as the by-product of grace.

In conclusion, *Grace for Living* includes all of God's provisions for daily living which are necessary for survival in this lifetime. We don't earn them nor deserve them. They are available on the basis of God's grace-attitude.

Summary

1. Our life-styles are related to the many details of life.
2. These details of life make up God's provisions for daily living in the world.
3. Each detail is important and plays a vital role in our lives.
4. We don't earn them or deserve them. They are here to meet our needs.
5. Therefore, they are not to be our source of happiness.
6. Since we represent Jesus Christ in the world, we must learn how to relate to the abundance of things properly.
7. We have the option of human viewpoint or divine viewpoint toward the details of life.
8. From human viewpoint, we will be mastered by the details of life, and we will fail to enjoy them as God's grace provisions.
9. From the divine perspective, we will master the details of life, and therefore, we will enjoy them to the fullest.

4

Dependent Availability

Jesus' substitutionary victory over sin and separation from God is not just "pie in the sky by and by." It can also serve as our strength and stay in every situation. We need to learn to capitalize daily on God's *Grace-for-Living* provisions. The key is dependent availability on the indwelling Holy Spirit's control which assures us of the proper divine perspective.

Through our availability to what God has made available to us, Jesus can become our vitality for liberated living. In each day's deliberations, we can be *his* voice, *his* visibility, and serve as *his* vehicle of value.

What glorious gems of truth for the believer to contemplate every morning as he moves out into the heat of the day! What a privilege to penetrate life's knotty knolls, miserable mountains, and pleasant pastures knowing that we are positioned forever in the plan of God. What encouragement and divine energy is released when we are positive to his purposes.

The Equipment for Battle

Even though as believers we are positioned forever in the plan of God with heaven assured, we have a serious problem. We were created by God to live in mental unity, moral completeness, and physical fullness. This is possible because we have the indwelling Holy Spirit who is adequate for every confrontation.

We also have another nature—a lower nature—residing in our thinking. Because of this sin nature, the quality of our daily living will often fall far short of what God has provided. Dependent availability becomes difficult. We will fail to enjoy anything like the confidence which is available for us. "Now if I do what I do not desire to do, it is no longer I doing it—it is not myself that acts—but the sin [principle]

51

which dwells within me [fixed and operating in my soul]" (Rom. 7:20).

Instead of mental unity, we find that disharmony and frustration often hound us. Rather than moral completeness, perversions and inconsistencies plague us. Physical fullness may seem like an impossibility because we are so unhappy mentally. Every believer is a mental battleground. We have two natures, the new nature in Christ and the sin nature, which vie for control over our thinking. Each nature desires to be our controller in each situation we encounter. In addition, we have a free will which allows us to decide which controller will dominate our thinking.

A description of the battle is given in Galatians 5:16–18. This passage encourages us to allow the Holy Spirit to control our thinking. This indicates volition. Paul stated that with the Holy Spirit in control of our minds, we will not entertain the cravings of the sin nature. He pointed out that the sin nature and the Holy Spirit are enemies, constantly warring against one another.

Paul dealt with the negative, destructive attitudes which are manifested when the sin nature is in control (vv. 19–21). He claimed that the practices of this anti-God nature will be obvious in our behavior. These sin-nature activities may run the gamut from immoral actions to severe revenge tactics to harsh complaining and criticizing. When such behavior is evidenced, it proves that we are not under the Holy Spirit's control.

Then verses 22–23 present the positive results which are evidenced when the Holy Spirit is in control of our thinking. They are love, joy, peace, patience, kindness, goodness, faithfulness, gentleness, and self-control. So the battle rages between the sin nature and the new nature in Christ (under control of the Holy Spirit) in the believer's mind. It is real and must be dealt with constantly.

The amazing truth is that we have all the needed equipment through the grace-provisions of God. That equipment is the indwelling Holy Spirit and the written Word of God. It is only through the control of the Holy Spirit that we can cope successfully with the sin nature. But this knowledge of the sufficiency of the Holy Spirit doesn't assure us that we will relax into his control. This is where the written Word serves as a vital vehicle to our lives. As we live on a balanced banquet of Bible knowledge, the Holy Spirit has the needed information to encourage us to allow him to control our thinking.

We can bask in the fantastic truth that the battle is the Lord's and not our own. We will realize that we cannot handle sin in our own strength. Whenever we try, we fail and increase our own misery and frustration. The Christian life is present tense. The battle is moment by moment and situation by situation. Only God can deal with the sin nature and forgive sin. When we relax mentally into God's control, he wins the battle over sin. The by-product for us will be peace of mind and mental stability. Our responsibility is to be God's yielded instrument.

Satan's Energy Fallout

Battles are fought on battlegrounds. Often we attempt to win the fight against the sin nature in our own strength. This is an impossible task. To deal with this anti-God influence apart from the Holy Spirit's control is foolish. For this reason, many times we experience an energy fallout or a quality loss as we move from the worship service to the workbench. Somehow, there seems to be a breakdown in spiritual energy and effectiveness which takes place between the Bible class and the business desk. We seem to fail in confidence from the *koinonia* fellowship to the kitchen sink. We are ever listening and claim to be learning, but when we need to apply what we know about God, we are helplessly unprepared. In reality, a loss of power develops between the inspiration of the worship service and the perspiration of the workaday world.

We are obligated to function in a world of anti-God thinking. We may learn many Bible promises and principles in the formal church classroom. But we seem to lose what it takes to successfully cope with the pressures and crises which we face on life's firing line. The basic reason for this energy waste and the breakdown of God-power-effectiveness is carnal living. Carnality means that we are controlled by the sin nature. In carnality, we are operating on our own, apart from God's control. It is Satan's filter system which weakens every aspect of our Christian witness and tends to neutralize the power which Christ is in us.

Let's examine some of the ways carnality can render us weak and ineffective believers. Apart from the release of the Holy Spirit to fill us, our Christian lives will be dull, monotonous, and boring. When we are carnal, we can become bogged down in church activities and religious functions in the name of Christ. We can boast of our activities, go through all the proper motions of Christian living, but it is all a form of godliness with no heavenly force. We will be putting on a front—a facade—and we are faking it. We are like the clothing store manager who has all his merchandise in the store window but nothing in stock. There is no spiritual reserve based on God's Word.

Day after day we can perform mechanically, conforming to man-made patterns with very little profit to anyone. Our Christian witness and life-styles will be dry and uninteresting. We will be sustained but not satisfied. Our circumstances may force us to go through the motions of Christian service, but we will be bored to death in the process. There will be little enthusiasm and excitement evidenced in our endeavors. This pattern can lead to willful rebellion and disobedience.

Furthermore, we will be haunted by a secret desire to escape it all. Yet guilt will move in with any attempt to flee, because we are afraid of what others will think. We may avoid any thoughts about God being present in us. Since we cannot run from him, we may willfully attempt to resist his claims on our lives. Yet, we will experience fear, wondering if he will forsake us. This keeps our souls in constant conflict, and we may even go to sleep afraid that we may not wake up the next morning.

Because of Satan's filter system of carnality, we can find ourselves in all sorts of mischief and idolatry, mentally and physically. We will yield to the pressure of our circumstances. As a result, we will be controlled by despair and misgivings. Our testimony will be dull. Any excitement and enthusiasm will be short-lived. In addition, Satan's filter system may cause our vision to grow dim and any light of encouragement to vanish.

In carnal living, we will not know what we need. So we will spend much time searching for what we think we want. We will seek to please ourselves, rather than Jesus. We will live in self-imposed poverty even though we may have an abundance of things. God will be quenched and grieved. Therefore, he is prevented from giving us what we need, while we are impoverished by what we want to think.

Carnality is not a happy way to live. We will grumble more than we rejoice. As a part of our defenses, we will act like we have all that it takes to be a successful person apart from God. We will refuse to remember what we know. Instead we will remember what God forgets.

So many believers seem to think that true Christian maturity comes from what they accomplish for God in their own strength. Yet, they are disappointed most of their lives because they are negative to God's Word. They fail to release the Holy Spirit to accomplish in and through them all that God demands. We represent Jesus Christ on earth. But in order to be effective and do the will of God, we must know the mind of Christ. However, satanic influence through our sin natures will seek to contradict any need of Bible information. It will try to impress upon us that we are not as bad as the Bible makes us out to be. Also, our sin natures will try to point out all that is good in what we are, apart from what Christ is. We may entertain such thoughts as, God takes things too far. He judges too sternly. His sentences are unwarranted. He exaggerates the issue.

With this attitude, we are functioning on our own and will have to decide what is good or bad, right or wrong. We may argue that certain actions are improper. But we will refuse to admit our sin-nature depravity, and that we are spiritually bankrupt. You see, the sin nature doesn't want to be exposed. Therefore, in our attempts to disguise our sin natures, it can influence us to hurt others, to offend our friends, and to be indignant and resentful toward our loved ones. At the same time, we will seek to justify our actions. Yet, we will see no inconsistency in our behavior, and we may even assume an air of offended innocence. We will claim to be reasonable, sensible, logical, and economical as we try to dedicate to God our self-life, which God has crucified.

We may seek to spare the sin nature, but it will never spare us. We may claim that there is good in it, and we can spend much time and effort trying to domesticate it and make it presentable to God. But it never works.

In carnality we don't always desire to be evil. We may try desperately to please God. But we can't seem to get through to him. We go to church, but so often there is no awareness of God. We can give our tithes, our time, and our talents in Christian service but refuse to release him in our minds and bodies. We can major on the right religious things, pray spasmodically, and claim to live by faith, but things seem to master us. Our praying doesn't connect us with God, and our faith seems to be mere wishful thinking.

We may have a quantity of religious deeds but no quality of divine power. We are the salt of the earth, but we have lost our savor. We are alive spiritually but live a nonproductive life. We are like a dry fountain, beautifully constructed with no supply of water to refresh ourselves or others. We may be grateful to God and experience a strong urge to follow him, but we eventually come to terms with the sin nature. As a result, we continue to compromise and practice our pet religious habits which are contrary to God's Word and plan for our lives.

The tragedy is that we have available all that God is in wealth and grace provisions, yet we live in spiritual poverty. We can become so comfortable in carnality that we don't want to get out. Even though we enjoy a measure of success in our church functions, we are lacking in spiritual substance.

We need to learn that every hour we spend in carnality, we are defrauding ourselves of the victorious living-grace provisions that Christ won for us on the cross. We must learn that we have lived in carnality long enough.

It's amazing how carnal thinking can cause us to ignore what we sing about God from the hymn books. We can easily forget what we say about him and never listen to how we pray. We can even live as if he were dead. It's shameful to say, but when we are carnal, most of what is produced in our thinking and behavior is unacceptable to God. Our life-styles will be explained only in terms of our own ability and power. What we really lack is a release of God's power. We have his power in us, waiting to be released, but we are not yielded to him.

When we fail to surrender to the Holy Spirit's control, we are under the influence of Satan's filter system and we get in God's way. Our lives are not free-flowing channels of his love. Thus, we become unworthy representatives of Jesus Christ. We become enslaved by our own self-efforts for God and entangled in the cares of the world. "As for what was sown among thorns, this is he who hears the Word, but the cares of the world and the pleasure *and* delight *and* glamour *and* deceitfulness of riches choke *and* suffocate the Word, and it yields no fruit" (Matt. 13:22).

In our church activities we may find ourselves suffering bitterly in the maze of programs and God is not glorified. The sin nature will inflict us with guilt because we are unable to do what we think we should be doing for God. At the end of each endeavor for Jesus, we will face the disturbing questions: Was it worth it? Did I accomplish anything worthwhile? Apart from the Holy Spirit's control, God is unable to touch others in and through us. And he cannot fill us with his peace of mind and mental stability.

We will be plagued with that empty-of-God feeling and that helpless, hopeless awareness that we are spiritually bankrupt. In carnality, all the power and adequacy that Christ is in us and all the Bible principles and promises to which we are exposed can become a waste in experiential living. The details of *Grace for Living* become our reason for living instead of an opportunity for celebrating our relationship with God.

God's Energy Booster

In contrast to carnality, God has a booster system called spirituality. Spirituality means that the Holy Spirit is in control of our thinking. As a result, we become overflowing channels of godliness. The gifts of the Spirit come to the surface of our behavior, and the harmony of the church is enhanced. All who cross our pathway become aware of our demonstration of Christ's miraculous way of life, because we are evidencing in our behavior the fruit of the Holy Spirit.

God didn't design us to remain spiritually destitute and defeated in the experiential world. He has provided for us the capacity and the procedure to remember what we know as we face life. The procedure is to rest in dependent availability on him, claim his promises, and release his presence by faith. As a result, everything that is possible for him becomes possible for us in the confines of his will. His strength, wisdom, and drive replace our weakness, folly, and defeat. Our greed is conquered by his grace. Our problems evaporate before his peace. Our lust is neutralized by his power. Our fears are subdued by his love. These spiritual blessings become operational because we are allowing him to stabilize us mentally. We are thinking soundly from the perspective of love and power. "God did not give us a spirit of timidity—of cowardice, of craven and cringing and fawning fear—but [He has given us a spirit] of power and of love and of calm *and* well-balanced mind *and* discipline *and* self-control" (2 Tim. 1:7).

It is God's purpose that we live under the Holy Spirit's control.

From this divine perspective, we realize that we are identified with Christ forever. We have become children of God, and we are partakers of his divine nature. In the royal family of God we are "sealed unto the day of redemption." The Holy Spirit makes the Bible come alive as we yield our entire personalities in availability to him. In the state of spirituality, we realize that the battle in us does not rest with us, but with God. Further, as we lean in total dependence upon the Holy Spirit, he will celebrate in us the victory already won. We move out of the shadows of carnality into the reality of power. With his transformation, rivers of living water will begin to flow in and out of our lives. And we will begin to discover some of the grace-provisions which God has been providing all the time.

With the Holy Spirit released in our minds, we can refuse to compromise, to disobey God, and to worry. We remember what God has taught us. We enjoy the grace-benefits of our new life. When he is released, we begin to center our praying on celebrating what we have and are receiving instead of what we would like to get. Since the sin nature is out of the way, we can return to the basic truths of the Bible and allow God to be in us all we need for life.

In the spiritual status, every day we enjoy new plateaus, and every experience is like a new chapter. Our language becomes the evidence of mental victory. Our faith becomes infectious as we manifest spiritual reserve and allow the Holy Spirit room to work in our thinking. We can be still and know that he is God. We don't have to panic or be anxious about anything. We can willingly go God's way, live one day at a time, and relax into his victory. In spirituality, we realize that he is all we need. We don't seek what we already have. So we have the grounds on which to celebrate our relationship with him. We begin to enjoy the living grace-provisions we have had all along from God's divine perspective. We refuse to make our plans, hoping that God will approve. We realize that our life is God's problem. Instead of begging him to take sides with us, we will allow him to take us over.

The energy fallout can be greatly minimized when Christ's sufficiency and stability are released in our thinking. This needed mental stability comes from our relationship with God. It is realized whenever the Holy Spirit is released to be in us all that God demands of us as his disciples. In this manner, our activities can become God's avenues to accomplish through us his own work.

As a result, we discern rightly the concepts of *Grace for Living* and how we are to relate properly to the details of life. We will realize that we have as our potential everything we need for any situation. "His divine power has bestowed upon us all things that [are requisite and suited] to life and godliness, through the (full, personal) knowledge of Him Who called us by *and* to His own glory and excellence (virtue)" (2 Pet. 1:3). Then, as we seek and apply the mind of Christ from the Word of God, we will become living demonstrations of the life of God. Furthermore, as the Holy Spirit is released to monopolize our thinking, we will do the will of God and teach the ways of God. God has provided for us unlimited quantities of his power. Our responsibility is to release that power by faith in the fact of his Word. Believing and living in the Word of God must become our way of life. This is dependent availability.

The Example of Christ

As we become aware of the vast areas of grace-provisions, how can we relate to them in dependent availability? The answer is found in the example Christ is to us. The kind of life which Christ lived while here on earth is our example of the quality of life and commitment God intends for us to live. That quality of life is our total dependence and availability to God the Holy Spirit. "So Jesus answered them by saying, I assure you, most solemnly I tell you, the Son is able to do nothing from Himself—of His own accord; but He is able to do only what He sees the Father doing. For whatever the Father does is what the Son does in the same way [in His turn]" (John 5:19).

With this kind of attitude our relationship to the details of life will be proper and wholesome. Jesus' example challenges us that just as he lived on earth in total availability to the Father, to live in and through him, we are to be available to the Holy Spirit so he may live the life of Jesus in and through our lives. This is how we please God and fulfill his just demands.

"When you have lifted up the Son of man [on the cross], you will realize (know, understand) that I am He [for Whom you look]; and that I do nothing from Myself—of My own accord, or on My own authority—but I say [exactly] what My Father has taught Me.

"And He Who sent Me is ever with Me; My Father has not left Me alone, for I always do what pleases Him" (John 8:28–29).

In *Grace for Living*, God has provided all the details of life needed to keep us alive in this world of anti-God thinking. They are his provisions for our daily living. As we grow in grace-orientation through the knowledge of Christ, we begin to discover some of the fantastic things which God has been doing, is doing, and will continue to do in and through us. We will discover that each day, as well as all that accompanies it, is in some way related to the grace of God. In addition, all of our circumstances can be considered as being influenced directly or indirectly by God's grace-provisions for salvation and daily living.

Summary

1. The proper relationship to the details of *Grace for Living* is dependent availability.
2. We are a battleground. The battle is between the sin nature and the Holy Spirit.
3. We make the decision as to which controller will dominate our thinking—the sin nature or the Holy Spirit.
4. The indwelling Holy Spirit is our only defense against the sin nature.
5. When we are carnal, we are controlled by the sin nature. This causes a great waste of divine power.
6. When we are spiritual, we are controlled by the Holy Spirit. This provides a divine booster to enhance miraculous living in and through our behavior.
7. The battle is not ours, but the Lord's.
8. When we are Spirit-controlled, we win the battle over the sin nature; and God's living grace-provisions become a blessing.

Part III
Greater Grace

We have studied God's grace-provisions for salvation and daily survival. Now as we continue to explore God's garden of grace-information, we discover that there is *much more*. We shall call this area of grace, *Greater Grace*. It is the capacity to recognize, receive, and enjoy many of the grace-provisions which God has made available beyond mere survival. Our two areas of discussion will be, "New Capacity" and "Provisions, Promotions, and Prosperity."

5

New Capacity

As we relate to the details of *Grace for Living*, we will either use them wisely or become their slaves. But God has provided more than just enough to sustain us and to keep us alive in the world. The "much more" of God's grace package includes God's provisions which are beyond the stage of *Grace for Living*. They can belong only to those who are willing to consistently grow in grace-orientation through maximum Bible study and application. "But He gives us more and more grace [power of the Holy Spirit, to meet this evil tendency and all others fully]" (Jas. 4:6).

God's *Greater Grace* is the ultimate in victorious Christian living. It is that God-given capacity to appreciate all that God desires to give. In *Greater Grace*, we move into the realm of spiritual rest and availability. We are avenues of maximum production for God. This is possible because we are united in our minds on the basis of Bible principles. We are not tossed to and fro by every wind of doctrine and adverse circumstance of life.

This ability can be called a positive mental attitude, a spiritual building, or a cup. It is solely the gift of God. Through concentrated Bible study and consistent Bible-based thinking under the control of the Holy Spirit, we will feed the written Word to the indwelling, living Word. As a result, he will construct this positive mental capacity in the soul. We will live and think on the basis of grace. We will have a relaxed mental attitude in all situations. We will have the divine capacity to evidence a right attitude of love in all our relationships. There will be no hate, worry, fear, or anxiety in our thinking. We will be relaxed with God's mental stability and confidence in the face of all the pressures and sufferings of life. It is from this quality of mentality that we can be launched into the orbit of superabundant grace-living.

"The thief comes only in order that he may steal and may kill and may destroy. I came that they may have *and* enjoy life, and have it in abundance—to the full, till it overflows" (John 10:10). God the Holy Spirit is able to develop in us that mental capacity to receive the super grace-blessings which God is waiting to pour out on us.

As a result, our spiritual cups will overflow with an overcoming life-style. We will demonstrate a dynamic witness for Jesus Christ. This witness will be represented in and through our daily lives. Wherever we go, we will be the salt of the earth and the light of the world. Furthermore, our behavior becomes an embarrassment to Satan because our lives will evidence a confident, conquering, and consoling joy amid every pressure and problem.

In the previous section, we learned that in God's *Grace for Living*, our volition is not involved in the availability of the details of life. However, in *Greater Grace*, our free wills determine the quantity of super-grace-blessings which God can pour into our spiritual cups. When our attitudes toward God and his Word are negative, the Holy Spirit is grieved and quenched. God can't pour out his blessing. But when we are positive in attitude, God can release in us his fantastic happiness and mental stability. This proper mental attitude is important in the enjoyment of God's *Greater Grace* provisions.

A Breakthrough

God has made all that he is available to the believer. The issue is not, "Is God available?" but "Are we available to him?" Consider what is involved in arriving at the mental attitude which will introduce us to this valley of victory called *Greater Grace*.

The first step is a complete breakthrough. This spiritual breakthrough consists of our awareness and assurance that God's power and stability are available and adequate for every confrontation. The arrival at this plateau of faith is essential to bring us to a total abandonment of our own self-efforts. Only then will we recognize that everything must be faith-rested into the Holy Spirit's control.

As we study the life of Jesus, it is interesting to note how often the disciples faced a dilemma and failed to realize the power which was available to them in Christ Jesus. One such encounter is the feeding of the five thousand. Let's review this story from the perspective of Christ's availability. In this incident there are three conversations worthy of investigation.

The First Conversation (Mark 6:34–37)

This conversation is between Jesus and his diciples. Jesus had been teaching the people for a long time. It was late afternoon. The people were hungry, and there was no food. The disciples faced an impossible situation. They came to Jesus with their answer to the dilemma. It was, "Send them away." How often do we face impossible situations, and the only solution we can think of is to avoid our responsibilities?

In verse 37, Jesus gave them his solution, "Give ye them to eat" (KJV) Now, there were over five thousand people to feed. How could a small band of followers feed all of them? The issue was not how they could accomplish this feat. The issue is what Jesus was trying to teach them.

They faced an impossible situation from the human perspective. Jesus Christ, representing all the power of God, was available. But on whom were the disciples depending? Were they depending on Jesus? No! Jesus was available to them, but they were *not available* to him. This same Jesus is also available and adequate for every situation we face. If we refuse to be available to him, we will fail to be his vehicle of *Greater Grace* blessings. In addition, we will miss out on the by-product of his peace of mind and mental stability.

The Second Conversation (John 6:5–7)

This conversation is between Jesus and Philip. Jesus asked Philip a question, "Whence shall we buy bread, that these may eat?" (KJV) Why did Jesus do this? He already knew everything about Philip. "He himself knew what he would do" (v. 6, KJV). Jesus asked the question because he was trying to teach Philip that he was and is available. In verse 7, we find Philip's answer, "Two hundred pennyworth of bread is not sufficient for them, that every one of them may take a little" (v. 7, KJV).

Philip was saying that this was an impossible situation, and he was right. But he was thinking from the human perspective, on the basis of material resources. Now, on whom was Philip depending? Neither Philip nor the other disciples were depending on Jesus. Jesus was available to them, but they were *not available* to him.

How often do we face humanly impossible situations and fail to realize that Jesus is available and adequate to stabilize us in that crisis? We may claim to be believers, but we talk and live as if we were atheists. We can fail to be available to all that God has made available to us. So, we will struggle with our problems. We will fight those dearest to us. We may burden ourselves down with such attitudes as worry, fear, guilt, and hostility.

During these periods of carnality, we are unsuccessful in coping with any situation. The point is that we have his power to face everything victoriously. But that power must be acknowledged as we face the pressures and problems of life.

The Third Conversation (John 6:8–14)

This conversation is between Andrew and a small boy. This boy had a lunch consisting of five barley loaves and two small fishes. We can imagine that the conversation was initiated by the lad. "Mister, please take me to your Master. I have a lunch, and I want to help Jesus feed these people." Perhaps Andrew was reluctant at first. However, after much persistence on the lad's part, Andrew took him to Jesus. He said, Master, "there is a lad here, which hath five barley loaves, and two small fishes: but what are they among so many?" (v. 9, KJV).

Now on whom was Andrew depending? Did he believe that Jesus could do anything? Evidently, to Andrew, the boy's lunch was a joke. But in response to the lad, Jesus said, "He's the one I'm looking for. He thinks I can do something. Make the people sit down." Now what is the lesson? This lad's attitude teaches us how to face every routine, responsibility, and relationship in the *Greater Grace* capacity. Again, the key is to know and to acknowledge that God's power is available and adequate for every situation. This is the breakthrough.

The Bankruptcy

Once we move into the awareness of God's availability and adequacy, the next step is to declare spiritual bankruptcy. This declaration of spiritual poverty is the positive response needed to enjoy superabundant living. The concept of bankruptcy is that we come to the end of trusting in our self-life. Rather, we expose every facet of our lives to Christ's adequacy.

In declaring spiritual bankruptcy, we discover a capacity to enjoy what God has and is providing. As our spiritual I.Q. reaches maturity, we will have a maximum amount of Bible knowledge. As a result, we will begin to live a life-style which can only be explained in terms of Christ living in and through our behavior. Thus, we begin to enjoy our freedoms. We begin to give ourselves in love and service to God with no strings attached.

To indicate how vital it is to relax into God's control, let us examine some negative possibilities. If we fail to discover the breakthrough of God's availability and declare spiritual bankruptcy, our abilities to function in the workaday world and our church activities may intrude in on God's purpose for our lives. We may be attracted to religion and legalism. From the legalistic approach, we may be tempted to use our talents and abilities to set up gimmicks and escape routes to manipulate God. In our attempt to avoid some specific Christian service to our neighbor, we may approach Christian living on the basis of our own rights. We will tend to consider our everyday routines and professions as separated from our relationship with God.

So often, some believers try to give the impression that they have the Christian life tied up in a neat little package. They try to carry their Christianity around like a credit card for emergency use. They seem to think of God's presence as their spiritual life insurance policy which they can file away for future use as the need arises.

In the meantime, they will try to go on in their system of religious works and spiritual taboos and church functions. They will pick out the things which the church offers that meet their own ego needs. As a result, they are not totally committed to Jesus. Their quality of Christianity is reduced to an organized attempt to be God's public-relations experts with a flashy smile, a glad handshake, and the proper pious platitudes. Their unhappiness and hypocrisy is hidden most of the time by a veneer of Christian vocabulary such as "Brother," "Praise the Lord," "Pray about it," and so on. This approach to Christian living often serves only to give off a foul spiritual odor to God and is offensive to most unbelievers, as well as some believers.

The point is that apart from declaring spiritual bankruptcy, our entire system of religion collapses. When a crisis arises, we will be forced to rely on our own limited abilities to cope with it. We may try to impress God by using our spiritual credit card of works. We may try to cash in our legalistic insurance policy of rules, regulations, and taboos in order to make demands of God.

With this carnal approach, God is unable to provide his mental stability. Also, if we continue to avoid spiritual bankruptcy, we may try to salvage some sense of stability by doubling our efforts in repeating Scriptures and "hustling" for God. But there will be no *Greater Grace* victory. Instead, our physical endeavors and attempts at autosuggestion can become a psychological way to bribe God.

We may use such functions as teaching, preaching, and witnessing as an attempt to sell God on the idea that he ought to come through for us in ways that stimulate our own selfish desires. So often, we fail to realize that God's grace, in every stage, rejects the activities of the sin nature. We may forget that we bring nothing to God but ourselves, and if we are not available vessels for his use, the Christian life doesn't work for us. So, until we declare spiritual bankruptcy, we will live in mental frustration. Instead of the Christian life being a relaxed adventure, it will be a struggle all the way.

Christianity is a relationship with God which doesn't depend on our own personalities; the capacity for victorious miraculous living can only be tapped through declaring spiritual bankruptcy as each situation, crisis, or problem arises moment by moment.

The Brokenness

Many believers fail to realize all that God has provided for them experientially. They become so busy hustling around the church community seeking satisfaction that they ignore God's perfect peace, strength, and mental stability which are true happiness. They make a lot of noise and impress a few people but those to whom they minister find very little help in coping with their conflicts on marriage or the frustrations and pressures of the business world. There are a host of wonderful believers who can talk the language of salvation, but they are not happy Christians. Their attempts to please God often serve only to reveal their dread and boredom. Therefore, many times they will imitate unbelievers trying to find stimulation and to make their daily living palatable. Usually they are forced to use many of the same substitutes which the unbeliever uses to make it through a day.

These unhappy Christians are not consciously aware of God's presence in them, and they are negative to the written Word. So, they fail to relate what they know about God to their daily experiences. They may play out their Christian lives in such roles as pastors, missionaries, denominational workers, deacons, or Sunday School teachers. They help to make up the rolls of many local congregations. But they are tired and overwhelmed inwardly with a sense of defeat and futility. There seems to be a dichotomy between their Christian profession and their experiential living. They may smile sweetly, shake hands with vigor, and give some words of encouragement. However, all they do or say has a ring of shallow pretense.

Many of us can identify with this life-style. There are times when we bravely present a front which evidences the Christian life, but it's expressed out of a sense of duty. Expressions of love and devotion may be manifested in our actions. But they are forced from a feeling of obligation. Like the elder brother in the story of the prodigal son, there are times when we associate happiness with being away from our heavenly Father's influence. We may consider "fun" to be found in activities which are totally contrary to Bible-based Christianity. We can even anticipate with great joy making merry with our "friends" rather than serving as demonstrations of divine production.

So we are exhausted spiritually. Many times we feel that we are at the end of our spiritual endurance. We often may wonder, How can I please Jesus and still be happy? This is a tragic attitude because, regardless of the difficulties, pressures, circumstances, adversities, or problems we face, we can experience God's peace which transcends all understanding. "God's peace [be yours, that tranquil state of a soul assured of its salvation through Christ, and so fearing nothing from God and content with its earthly lot of whatever sort that is, that peace] which transcends all understanding, shall garrison *and* mount guard over your hearts and minds in Christ Jesus" (Phil. 4:7). This is true because God has provided his peace and the power which can make our lives count for him in the midst of every confrontation and tribulation.

Sooner or later, every believer must face the question: Now that I have trusted Jesus Christ for the big thing—salvation—can I trust him to give me stability in the everyday vexations and pressures of life? The answer is yes! We can depend on him for mental stability in the everyday problems, just as we depend on him for salvation. The issue is to come to the place of complete dependent availability upon the adequacy of God the Father. "As you have therefore received the Christ, [even] Jesus the Lord, [so] walk—regulate your lives and conduct yourselves—in union with *and* conformity to Him" (Col. 2:6).

However, we will not in our own efforts find that attitude of total trust which releases God's *Greater Grace* blessings. God has to bring us to the mental place of brokenness and spiritual bankruptcy. There are two specific ways through which God can bring us to brokenness.

First there is the hard way. This procedure is called discipline. There will be times when we are negative and carnal in our thinking about God. As a result, we will fail to cooperate with him. And he will be compelled to bring us to dependence through spiritual spanking. It is for our own good that God disciplines us when we are carnal. He has to protect us from our sin natures. We can be assured that when we fail to operate under the Holy Spirit's control, we will be disciplined.

God's discipline doesn't mean loss of salvation. God deals with us as children on the basis of his love. Also, discipline doesn't imply that God is mean and deliberately causing bad things to happen. Instead, he uses the situations and circumstances we face as tests to bring us to confession and dependence on him. By means of confession, he can turn discipline into blessing.

"If we [freely] admit that we have sinned *and* confess our sins, He is faithful and just [true to His own nature and promises] and will forgive our sins (dismiss our lawlessness) and continuously cleanse us from all unrighteousness—everything not in conformity to His will in purpose, thought and action" (1 John 1:9).

How can we avoid God's discipline? Here are some suggestions. Develop a positive attitude toward God the Father. Learn how to faith-rest each situation into God's control as it arises. This means that we ask God the Holy Spirit to take control of our thinking as we relate to that experience. Live under occupation with Christ. The idea here is to live in the Word of God, believing and thinking what we have learned as our way of life. Allow Bible promises and principles to condition your thinking as you relate to decisions and relationships. In this way, you can organize your thinking on the basis of Bible truth. You can seek to build every aspect of your life, your marriage, your business, and your social life on the principles of God's Word.

Attend Bible classes regularly under your pastor/teacher. Take notes and build a promise notebook so you can study later. Do not complain about repetition. To do so indicates that you have not yet learned the truth. On the other hand, once you really hear what is being taught, you will desire to hear it over and over.

Next, there is the easy way for God to bring us to dependence upon him. It is based on our positive attitude toward God and his written Word. In this approach, we hunger and thirst for Bible knowledge. We will organize and schedule our lives in such a way that we can study the Bible on a consistent basis. The result of this intake of Bible knowledge is that the Holy Spirit uses the needed information to teach us to depend on him willingly.

Once we really hear and learn a truth from God's Word, we will become self-sustained in it. So, we will not be required to learn it again. We shall never forget it. Also, we will desire to share it with anyone who will listen. In addition, God's Word is always fresh and exciting to the positive believer. Each time we are filled with the Holy Spirit, our relationship with God is refreshed and stimulated. The Holy Spirit takes the Bible information which we have stored in our minds to bring newness to every routine, responsibility, and relationship. As a result, our lives are never dull, and we are not bored.

This quality of faith-rest will allow the Holy Spirit to produce his divine works in and through our lives. In the activities of the Holy Spirit, our living faith will thrive. Because of our dependence upon the sufficiency of God and his Word, the Holy Spirit will release God's power through us to all who cross our pathways.

As a result, we will function effectively in our priesthood. Our giving, our worship, our praying, our singing, our preaching, our teaching, and our witnessing will become the activities of God the Holy Spirit released by our attitude of total availability. As "priests unto God," we will step out of mere existence into the realm of living grace, into superabundant living.

In *Greater Grace* living, we move from our weakness to God's power. We abandon our independence and make a total surrender. His joy replaces our sorrows. His plenty drives away our spiritual poverty. The awareness of his availability and adequacy strengthens our faith in him. We are able to cope with every pressure and blessing. Therefore, it is essential that we discover from the written Word that God is available and adequate for every phase of life.

This awareness is derived from only one source—the Bible. Thus, Bible information is used by the Holy Spirit to teach us, not only God's viewpoint about life, but also that only he is adequate to live the Christian life in and through us. Through Bible principles, the Holy Spirit is enabled to sustain us mentally in every situation. He will be able to guide us, to provide the needed confidence for life, and to give us the proper attitude of love toward others.

Summary

1. God has much more than *Grace for Living* available for us in this lifetime.
2. Our volition is involved. Therefore, to enjoy God's *Greater Grace* provisions, we must be positive in our mentality toward God and his Word.
3. First, God may be allowed to build in our minds a positive mental attitude.
4. The construction material which is essential for this kind of positive thinking is Bible knowledge stored in our minds.
5. The result will be a fantastic capacity to receive much of what God can pour out in terms of provisions, promotions, and prosperity.
6. Our lives will become avenues of witnessing and encouragement to all who cross our pathways.

6

Provisions, Promotions, and Prosperity

In these terrible times of testing when God's Word is being disputed, distorted, and diluted, is there any rhyme or reason to life? We may experience exciting exhilaration at the sealing of our salvation. We may be soundly satisfied with God's solution for sin. We can even live with the hope of heavenly happiness with God, where "death shall be no more" (Rev. 21:4).

But in the meantime, as we are buffeted by the bedlam of bad tempers, the breakdown of truths, and the barrage of things, can we really discover the deposits of God's quiet grace? As we battle with babies, budgets, and bifocals, can we know God's justice, jubilation, and joy on a consistent basis? Is there really a way to relate God's *Greater Grace* to our reason? Can we move beyond mere *Grace for Living* to where we master the mechanics of life?

The answer is an undeniable yes to the redeemed who realize how to receive God's *Greater Grace* reserve as their daily diet.

Greater Grace Available

God has made available his consoling comfort for every confrontation. This means that there are no situations or sets of circumstances for which he doesn't have the solution. God's method for solving every mountain of misery is to master us with his mental stability. Then, regardless of how the situation works out, we are not defeated. The spiritual handle to remember is that *Greater Grace* living is not a method to maneuver God; nor is it a technique to trick him into tolerating our tantrums. It is the normal Christian life, whereby we live on the basis of faith in the fact of God's Word. We deliberately depend on God's Word by relaxing into the indwelling, living Word's control and by the intake of his written Word. Through this process of cooperating with God, we have the capacity to capitalize on all that he

72

can provide. In this manner, he exchanges our weakness for his wealth. Thus, it's not just heaven someday, but God's presence and power now. This means that God's *Greater Grace* provisions provide a spiritual backbone for every frailty we face.

"But those who wait for the Lord—who expect, look for and hope in Him—shall change *and* renew their strength *and* power; they shall lift their wings *and* mount up [close to God] as eagles [mount up to the sun]; they shall walk and not faint *or* become tired" (Isa. 40:31).

Then we can move out every morning, knowing that we already have a good day ahead, regardless of any reverses, because of what we know about God.

"And my God will liberally supply (fill to the full) your every need according to His riches in glory in Christ Jesus" (Phil. 4:19).

"I have strength for all things in Christ Who empowers me—I am ready for anything and equal to anything through Him Who infuses inner strength into me, [that is, I am self-sufficient in Christ's sufficiency]" (Phil. 4:13).

In spite of these life-giving lessons from our living Lord, it seems that the most miserable, mixed-up members of the human race are born-again believers. They have been bought by Christ's blood and serve under his banner of blessings. They have the potential of being powerful generators of God's light for the world. But they are like dead dynamos, short-circuited by their self-centeredness and soul kinks.

Their involvement in the Christian community evolves on emotions and experiences. Their support has to be prodded and perpetuated by enlistment in extracurricular endeavors. Their faithfulness falters periodically unless they are hooked on functions designed to provide pep and to purposely pump up their interest.

Many are sincere in their service to activities. They indicate commitment to man-made creeds. They reflect indoctrination with some degree of theological intelligence. But they manifest a miserable life-style because they are mired in the merry-go-round of making a living while neglecting the *Greater Grace* life which is their only hope for liberty. In their folly, they fail to seek the inward motivation of sound, stabilized, Scripture-based thinking.

As a result, there is very little of the enlightening encouragement and excitement that has as its source the lessons of God's love. There is missing that essential evidence of experiential superabundant victory. On the positive side, they fail as avenues of God's *Greater Grace* promotions, provisions, and prosperity. They are not aware that all of their material merchandise and spiritual assets are a part of God's grace package.

The major motive of their ministry seems to be no more than a lifeless lip service to their Lord. All they seek to accomplish for him is limited to a sorry solicited support in a few functions of a local church fellowship. Their problem is not the church organization. Their hang-up is not denominational orthodoxy or even program orientation. These are essential in order to enhance the local church's efforts to establish her witness and effectiveness in the community. Also, the cause of their weakness is not church committees and the like. Rather, their problem is the control of the sin nature. This results in carnal living which is a negative indifference to God.

As a result of their wrong attitudes, they are inactive in serving him, ignorant of his Word, and ineffective in prayer. Because they are minus sufficient Scripture information and refuse the Holy Spirit's control on a consistent basis, God is unable to indoctrinate them with his viewpoint. This means that the Holy Spirit cannot create in them the concepts and capacity needed to collect God's provisions, promotions, and prosperity which he has prepared for them in his grace package. So they are victims *of* their circumstances rather than victorious *over* them.

They are like the athlete who practices with persistence but refuses to play in the game. They know the challenges of the Christian life, but they avoid becoming involved as available ambassadors. Their Christian experiences evidence little or no excitement and encouragement because they refuse to follow through in faith dependence. And they fail as avenues through which the all-sufficient Christ can flow.

Why are so many who bear the name of Jesus evidencing so much failure and frustration in applying God's grace-goodness to their lives? We have all the adequacy of God, alive and available to work in and through us. Then, why is there so much animosity and anxiety among Christ's ambassadors, when our very *name* implies that we are to imitate him?

There is no conclusive answer to this question. However, in my own Christian experience, understanding the principles of God's grace and recognizing and receiving his provisions have given me a dynamic *Reason for Joy*. As I relax in yieldedness to him and acknowledge his presence, the Holy Spirit is released in and through my life. He can reproduce the likeness of Christ in my behavior. I have discovered that it is essential that we grow in grace-understanding through the knowledge of God. Peter gave us the answer as he challenged us to "grow in grace."

"But grow in grace (undeserved favor, spiritual strength) and recognition *and* knowledge *and* understanding of our Lord and Savior Jesus Christ, the Messiah. To Him [be] glory (honor, majesty and splendor) both now and to the day of eternity. Amen—so be it!" (1 Pet. 3:18).

The question is not *if* God is available to us. He *is* available! The questions are: How available are we? What is the quality of our availability?

God's Greater Grace Activity

Not only is God's *Greater Grace* available, it is his very activity on our account. *Greater Grace* is God expressing himself in his excellency to evil men. His activity was actualized and made available on the cross. Christ's conquering on the cross allowed God to do for us all that we were unable to do for ourselves. He canceled out our debt and secured our salvation. He opened the door to the dungeon of sin. All who receive him as redeemer are rescued as a result of grace. In addition, Christ produced the potential of superabundant living for all who will accept him by faith. In order to enjoy and experience the Father's provisions, promotions, and prosperity, we must enter his plan by personal faith in Jesus Christ.

God's grace-activity, actualized on the cross, can have some intriguing implications. Actually, God's grace becomes our blessed assurance as we live in the Holy Spirit's liberty. This means that the Holy Spirit's presence can give us confidence in all our confrontations. His vicarious victory over sin and death is our vitality for life. This victory is verified when his love is released to master our mentality.

What is the result? We move beyond *Grace for Living* into receiving God's *Greater Grace* activities. We begin to fulfill our potential of being his powerful generators. God can use us to light the lives of others with his life. We can become, not dead, but living dynamos neutralizing the short circuits of self-centeredness. As we stand on God's promises, we become dynamic demonstrations of his cords of consoling love. Since we are fastened to his faithfulness by faith, we are separated from spiritual death. In addition, the sin nature can be conquered moment by moment. So we can discover daily deliverance from the curse of sin's control. As we can cooperate with God by faith, we can throw off our carnal robes of self-righteousness. We will become his avenues of witness. Our responsibility is to relax and rest mentally in the Holy Spirit's resources. The consequences for us will be complete confidence in all we face.

As we remain positive to God in the *Greater Grace* realm, we are self-sustained. We are possessed by a treasure house of continuing joy. Since we know that we are right with God, we become winsome witnesses for Jesus. Wherever we are, we can reveal a refreshingly radiant mentality that is relaxed. We can rejoice in everything because the self-life is set aside. We can laugh at tomorrow in the sense that we are qualified to cope successfully with anything.

We can move about in this world beyond the stage of mere living-grace, embarrassing the devil because we are joyful and undefeatable. We can also invade that wave of indifference which infiltrates so many of God's people, leaving with them a positive, inspiring influence. We can slice through the sluggishness of the comfortable church crowd, challenging them to commitment.

In all situations, we can manifest God's might. We can refuse to listen to the sin nature's lies. We can become God's divine enablers to interest others toward him through our availability to him.

As God's *Greater Grace* activity becomes an increasing reality, we can serve as his instruments of righteousness. We can stand in the gap between Holy God and sinful man.

God's Greater Grace Applied

The fact that God has made perfect provisions for all that we encounter is not wishful thinking. Actually, God doesn't desire for us to live in dull, defeated doldrums. We are not supposed to sneak through life singing the blues, a slave to any situation. The solution to any problem is not how it works out, but that we approach it with a positive mental attitude. Most people can be humanly happy when everything is working out to their advantage. Only a small percentage of our confrontations commence or conclude just as we planned. So we need a mentality that is mastered by rest and a relaxed stability in any of the crises and circumstances that gang up on us. This means that in order to cope successfully with any situation, we must be thinking straight. Now the essence of sound thinking is mental involvement in the right information.

At this point I face the question, "Is there any possible way for a mixed-up person to acquire a relaxed mental attitude in all of his ups and downs?" It is obvious that, left to our own efforts, we can't "cut it." The only solace we can salvage apart from God's provisions is to sweat it out in substitutes.

This is where God's grace-genius gives us hope. There is a God-given means to live with mental mastery, day by day, over the devil's world of anti-God madness.

The liberating lesson that every God-lover must learn is that God the Father is our only source for this mental mastery and soundness. His procedure is centered in the ministry of the Holy Spirit. From the moment of salvation, we have the Holy Spirit indwelling our lives. He is the only one who can give us a relaxed mental attitude in all situations.

In order for the Holy Spirit to provide mental stability, Bible riches must reside in us as his resources to regulate our mentality. The Holy Spirit uses the Bible principles which we have learned and believed as a means to build up in our thinking this positive mental capacity. As we faith-rest situations, allowing the Holy Spirit to master our minds, he is released to relate God's viewpoint to our thinking. Immediately he can bring to our remembrance the Bible truth that fits the situation. As a result, we are mentally stabilized in the problem. This is *Greater Grace* living.

We are undefeatable in that undertaking because the Holy Spirit has taken over our thinking. From Bible doctrines, he gives us divine discernment and spiritual common sense; and we can make definite decisions on the basis of God's viewpoint. We are enabled to say yes to the right things and no to the wrong things. We praise the Lord and keep on trusting him, regardless of the outcome. If the situation goes against us, we can accept it and avoid panic. If the situation goes in our favor, we will also praise the Lord. Furthermore, we can use that as a reason to rejoice about our relationship with God.

Without violating our volition, the Holy Spirit can lead us to pray effectively, to study the Bible, and to serve faithfully in functions of church leadership, all from the perspective of grace. In addition, we can exercize full stewardship of life and money. We can effectively minister to others. In this manner, the motivating ministry of the Holy Spirit makes real the saving life of Jesus, who is alive in us through the person and power of the Holy Spirit.

Our behavior can become an edifying evidence of Christlikeness to all those around us. We will be God's available sanctuaries through which he can express himself. We will be dependable and delightful to deal with in any responsibility of leadership. We will forsake the phony facade of formalized religious functions as the criterion to parade our Christian convictions. Instead, we will seek to do all "as unto the Lord." When we operate under his control, the by-product for our lives will be his power, protection, and peace of mind. We will recognize and enjoy many of God's provisions, promotions, and prosperity of *Greater Grace* living.

In addition, God will be able to pour out more and more provisions as we grow in the capacity to receive them. The key is a Bible-centered, positive, mental attitude, controlled by the Holy Spirit. There will be times when we will be negative and operating on human-viewpoint thinking. In those times, God will not be able to pour out his blessings. However, when we confess to God our carnal thinking, once again we will be back in the mental place of superabundant *Greater Grace*. Thus, we have a firm foundation and a *Reason for Joy* in all of our experience.

Summary

1. There are three stages of Christian growth: baby Christians, adolescent Christians, and mature Christians.
2. These stages are determined by the amount of Bible doctrine resident in our souls.
3. The danger zone is at the stage of adolescence.
4. Here we begin to have some fantastic experiences and victories over the pressures of life.
5. Therefore, it is very easy to think that we have arrived, and that we

no longer need to study the Bible or relax consistently in God's control.

6. However, there is so much more of God's grace-provisions available for the believer who is willing to move on to *Greater Grace* living.

7. If we are willing to continue on a crash program of Bible study under the Holy Spirit's control, he can construct in our minds the capacity to receive all that God can provide.

8. The greater our capacity, the more God can provide, because we can receive more.

9. However, until we move on to Christian maturity (the process of taking more and more Bible knowledge), God has to tap his foot, waiting for our willingness.

Part IV
Grace for Dying

In our mental journey through God's garden of grace, we have explored *Grace for Salvation*, *Grace for Living*, and *Greater Grace*. In the realization of God's grace package, we receive his riches for abundant living in this lifetime. But there is exciting evidence of an eternal existence beyond this world. The lesson that we will live eternally means that there is more to learn about God's grace than what he has provided for us here.

He has also promised all that is necessary for the successful encountering of that dramatic experience called death, which transfers us from this world of time into eternity. We shall call this provision, *Grace for Dying*. It is that God-given capacity to face the cessation of this lifetime with courage, confidence, and comfort. Our two areas of discussion will be, "Before Death Comes" and "The Time for Dying."

7
Before Death Comes

The moment we confessed Christ as Savior, we were identified with him forever. Heaven became our eternal home. Now, in this lifetime, as we grow in our understanding of grace through the knowledge of God's written Word, we acquire the awesome ability to receive God's glorious grace. Yet, there is more than the much more of *Greater Grace*. God's grace-riches also relate to our relationship with eternity.

The Protection of God

In our destiny with eternity, we deal with God. This fact can be a source of great strength.

We have related that all of God's grace-provisions depend on who and what he is. This means that God's grace has as its foundation, the fullness of his fixed faithfulness. His essence is our basis for protection through death, and for our survival beyond death. Let's summarize some essential characteristics of God's essence.

God Is Faithful

Every good gift and every perfect (free, large, full) gift is from above; it comes down from the Father of all [that gives] light, in [the shining of] Whom there can be no variation [rising or setting] or shadow cast by His turning [as in an eclipse] (Jas. 1:17).

God is incapable of, nor is he susceptible to, change of character. This means that he is always faithful. He will always keep his Word. His policies toward us will be determined by our volition-free will. God's character is immutable. We are blessed not on the basis of *our* activities and functions on his behalf, but on the basis of his faithfulness.

God Is Perfect Righteousness

"The Lord is [rigidly] righteous in all His ways, and gracious *and* merciful in all His works" (Ps. 145:17).

This means that God is perfectly glorified goodness. He has no sin, nor has he ever sinned. When we say that someone is good, we do it by comparing him with someone else. God can't be compared with his creation or with any of his creatures. He is perfect righteousness, and he has made his goodness beneficial for every believer. When we initially trusted Christ as Savior, God the Father imputed to us his innocence. Therefore, in this faith relationship, we can satisfy him, even though we are sinners. He recognizes that his righteousness is in us. Thus, we are liberated by God's life which is beyond death's destruction.

God Is Perfect Love

"And we know (understand, recognize, are conscious of, by observation and by experience), and believe (adhere to and put faith in and rely on) the love God cherishes for us. God is love, and he who dwells *and* continues in love dwells *and* continues in God, and God dwells *and* continues in Him" (1 John 4:16).

God-love is not a feeling that you have when you feel like you are going to have a feeling that you have never felt before. God-love is a perfect mental attitude. It is God placing value on the humanity and taking the initiative to give himself to mankind. His love is minus such negative thoughts as hate, worry, hostility, revenge, fear, and jealousy. This is God's actual attitude for all people, believers and unbelievers. God-love is his true motivation for mercy which results in his grace-actions toward us.

When God's love is released in the recesses of our thinking, we will become his messengers, motivated to ministry and service. Any reluctance concerning our rendezvous with death will be greatly reduced.

God Is Eternal Life

" 'Little children, keep yourselves from idols—false gods, [from anything and everything that would occupy the place in your heart due to God, from any sort of substitute for Him that would take first place in your life]' *Amen. So let it be*" (1 John 5:21).

Eternal life has no beginning, no ending. It is God's life that is the light of men. It was related to our lives at the moment of salvation. Once God's eternal life was established in us, the result was everlasting life. This means that as we approach the reality of death or become involved in consoling the bereaved, we know that God has established with us an eternal relationship which can't be broken.

God Is Perfect Sovereignty

"Know, recognize *and* understand therefore this day, and turn your [mind and] heart to it, that the Lord is God in the heavens above, and upon the earth beneath; there is no other" (Deut. 4:39).

God's sovereignty means that he is the supreme being of all the solar systems. He has always existed, and he always will. He has absolute authority over all aspects of his creation. He answers to no one. Whatever he does is perfect. When we trust him for salvation and depend on his stability in the face of our trials and temptations, we can go to no greater authority. He has perfect volition and has given to every person a free will. In the awareness of death, we relate to the One who cannot die. His life in us is his guarantee that he will prepare us for life beyond death.

"Now He Who has fashioned us (preparing and making us fit) for this very thing is God, Who also has given us the (Holy) Spirit as a guarantee [of the fulfillment of His promise]" (2 Cor. 5:5).

God Is Just and Fair

"And Peter opened his mouth and said: Most certainly *and* thoroughly I now perceive *and* understand that God shows no partiality *and* is no respecter of persons" (Acts 10:34).

It is impossible for God to be unfair to anyone. So his justice demands that he judge sin. Sin has to be paid for. Through his work on the cross, God's justice is satisfied and now he is just to forgive us our sins whenever they are confessed. Since we are believers, our sinning cannot disturb our assurance of life with him beyond physical death.

God Is All-knowing

"In Him all the treasures of [divine] wisdom, [of comprehensive insight into the ways and purposes of God], and [all the riches of spiritual] knowledge *and* enlightenment are stored up *and* lie hidden" (Col. 2:3).

This means that God is omniscient. Since he has and always will have all knowledge about us, we can trust him. He can only be fair in all his judgments. God's omniscience can be a terrible threat to the unbeliever and the carnal believer. It is a blessing to the spiritual believer who functions on Bible knowledge under the Holy Spirit's control. In relationship to death, he is aware of everything we must face.

God Is Everywhere

"Where could I go from Your Spirit? Or where could I flee from Your presence? If I ascend up into Heaven, You are there; if I make my bed in Sheol [the place of the dead], behold, You are there. If I take the wings of the morning and dwell in the uttermost parts of the sea, Even there shall Your hand lead me, and Your right hand shall hold me" (Ps. 139:7–10).

This means that God is omnipresent. He is in all places at the same time. Yet, he can relate to us in a unique personality with mind and will. We can't hide from his presence. He is always aware of us and interested in all that happens to us. His fantastic provisions which relate to life and death lose their effectiveness when we fail to be available to him.

God Is All-powerful

"For with God nothing is ever impossible, *and* no word from God shall be without power *or* impossible of fulfillment" (Luke 1:37).

God's omnipotence indicates his unlimited ability and authority. He has power to save us from sin, to establish us in a unique relationship with himself forever, and to keep us secure in that relationship and fellowship forever. He also has the authority and power to accomplish the Christian life in and through our yielded behavior. He can provide all his grace provisions and also apply them to our lives. Through faith, we can accept what God provides and say, Thank you.

His power and authority are personalized in us in the person of the Holy Spirit, the living Word. We learn to release his power through the intake of Bible knowledge, stored in our minds through concentrated Bible study. The Holy Spirit is the personal manifestation of God's power in our behavior. Bible information serves as the raw material which the Holy Spirit uses to stabilize us and to teach us God's divine viewpoint. This includes our involvement with death, whether it be our own or the death of another.

God Is Perfect Truth

"(Resting) in the hope of eternal life, [life] which the ever-truthful God Who cannot deceive, promised before the world *or* the ages of time began" (Titus 1:2).

God cannot lie nor even be in error about anything. He is our absolute standard. His truth is eternal and serves as our perfect criterion for life and death, by which he sustains us.

God's grace reveals that he provides his perfect provisions of grace for us now and throughout all eternity. His entire plan is based on his consistent character. As impeccable God, he can only have a perfect plan. This means that within his plan, we discover an everlasting protection which enlightens us of an existence beyond the experience of physical death. Remember, in facing death, we deal with the faithfulness of God the Father, God the Son, and God the Holy Spirit.

The Preparation by God

The finality of death and the fear of its encounter can present a powerful threat throughout our entire lives. Yet, the fear of death can be an advantage if it motivates us to accept his preparation for eternity. There are many Scriptures which signify God's personal preparation to fit us for death, even before we experience its reality. Psalm 23:4 teaches that God can remove from our minds any fear of death. But if we fail to believe Bible promises and refuse to relax in God's control, we may be as fearful of death as any unbeliever.

"Yes, though I walk through the [deep, sunless] valley of the shadow of death, I will fear *or* dread no evil; for You are with me; Your rod [to protect] and Your staff [to guide], they comfort me" (Ps. 23:4).

When the fear of death is fixed in our minds, we may imagine death many times before we actually experience it physically. We may reason that certain routines are reckless, such as holiday travel or flying. We may worry constantly about some dangers, real or imaginary, which seem to lurk about us. However, there is nothing in the Scriptures to suggest that we should fear death. Yet, so many believers have such an imagination that they can even experience nightmares concerning this supposed enemy.

In spite of the threats and pressures which death can generate, the believer who is under the Holy Spirit's control, with resident doctrine, can relate to death in a relaxed manner. We can know that God is with us, as we journey toward and through that valley of death, which the Scriptures call a shadow.

As we have indicated, in death, as well as in life, we are dealing with God and not with man. Also, our victory over death depends on who God is and what he has done through the finished work of Christ on the cross. This means that God has provided victory over death for all believers. Regardless of the kind of lives we have lived, when our time comes to die, we are children of God. He will take care of us in his own meaningful and merciful way. We can relax about death right now. He is with us before death, and we will be with him beyond death. Let's take note of the genius of God's preparing us for death.

1. *God prepares us for death through his deliverance in extreme difficulties.*

God begins his preparing us for death by establishing with us his eternal-life relationship. A real part of this relationship is our right response of faith which enables the Holy Spirit to give us God's joy and peace of mind. In addition to sharing God's mental stability, he meets our needs through the details of life. As we trust him, he can also deliver us mentally from any of the adversities of life. At times, God's deliverance will mean that he takes away the pressure entirely. But if he does not remove us from the source of suffering, he will provide the peace of mind, a right attitude, and his assurance amid the pressure or suffering. Furthermore, he can deliver us physically, if it is his will. In times of warfare, famine, and even when others say all manner of evil against us, we can have his peace of mind.

2. *Through Bible information, God can provide inner peace about physical death as we learn to rest mentally in him.*

It matters not if we are spiritual (controlled by the Holy Spirit), carnal (controlled by the sin nature), mature believers or immature believers, God is preparing us daily for physical death through his provisions for life. As we depend on God's grace-provisions day by day, we can cope. We can also accept his assurance as we anticipate actual death. The key is to function faithfully under the Holy Spirit's control.

When a believer is filled with the fear of death, he is also afraid of life. So it is a great mental victory when we can forsake the fear of death and face it with a firm and stable attitude. Why? Because God promises that, as we practice the principle of his presence, when death comes, we will not panic regardless of the circumstances. We will not be afraid of the activities which can cause death. This is possible because, from concentrated Bible study, we are cooperating with the Holy Spirit. He can provide for us God's perspective concerning death.

A normal Christian will not deliberately look for death. God fashioned us to live forever. However, when we realize the reality of death, whether it's from a natural cause, a narrow escape, or imagination, we can have complete confidence because we are under the Holy Spirit's control. In fact, until God has completed his purpose in and through a Spirit-controlled believer, the dangerous things in life cannot remove him from this lifetime. In addition, when God has finished with us here, nothing can keep us in this world. So we don't have to be afraid of death. Instead, we can stop fighting it and relax mentally and live in the confidence God can provide.

God relates to us one day at a time. When we awake each morning to begin a new day, there is no way of knowing what will happen during the day. Death may come at any moment. How we begin each day mentally can be the source of great comfort and strength. Here are some suggestions or which you can concentrate as you face each new day. It would be a good idea to make these ideas a part of your life-style. Before you throw back the covers or as you make preparation for the day, think these thoughts.

First: Thank you, Lord, for this new day. I don't deserve it, nor did I earn it. It is your grace-gift to me.

Second: Thank you, Lord, that I am still physically alive. This means that you still have a purpose for me in this world.

Third: Thank you, Lord, for the awareness that your will is to control my thinking as I live today. I am not required to search for what you want me to do. I am to relax mentally into your control.

Fourth: Thank you, Lord, that as I, by faith, allow you to control my thinking, you will accomplish your purpose in and through my routines, responsibilities, and relationships.

Fifth: Thank you, Lord, that as a result, You will pour out in me your three pro's of *Greater Grace* prosperity: provisions, promotions, and protection.

Sixth: Thank you, Lord, that you have made adequate provisions for every crisis which I will encounter today, even death.

Seventh: Therefore, thank you, Lord, for living in me. I know you love me and that I belong to you. Lord, I'm available. I'll go where you want me to go. I'll do what you want me to do. I'll be what you want me to be. I'll remember what I know about you as I live today.

Our mental attitudes about everything are so important. This is especially true as we anticipate death. The information we have in our minds determines our mental attitude. Therefore, with basic Bible information, we can begin each day with God. Moment by moment and situation by situation, we can faith-rest into God's control. To faith-rest a situation is to ask the Holy Spirit to take over our thinking in that encounter. Thereby we are not only prepared for life but we are also in the process of preparation for dying at all times. This indicates God's personal interest in each one of us. "Precious (important and no light matter) in the sight of the Lord is the death of His saints—His loving ones" (Ps. 116:15).

3. God prepares us for death as He provides comfort and strength for us who are left behind.

Life on earth does go on. Therefore, physical death does not stop the normal functions of the human race any more than it stops the believer's life with God. When we discover that we are dying, we shouldn't grieve that we are leaving loved ones behind. God will take care of them. To believe this relaxes and releases us from much fear and dread.

I was ministering to a Christian lady who was dying of cancer. She was thirty-four years old and had three lovely children. As we talked about her right relationship with God, she revealed a critical concern. "Pastor, I am a believer! I know that I'm going to a greater life. But I could face it all so much better if it were not for my children. You know that my husband is an alcoholic. I am so afraid that he will not take care of my babies."

Then, she asked a question that tested every fiber of her faith.

"Will God see to it that my children make it?" Because I had learned some Bible knowledge about God and death, we concluded with all confidence, "Yes, God will see to it that the children will make it." I pointed out that God had not failed her yet and suggested some Scriptures which substantiated God's faithfulness. I reminded her that he had cared for her and her family up to that moment. He would continue to be faithful to her children.

The husband did fail as she had feared. But God has done a marvelous job in ministering to the children because she was wise enough to leave with them a substantial supply of Bible secrets. Not only had she led each one to salvation through faith in Jesus Christ, but also she had demonstrated God's deliverance in her life by the manner in which she met the misery of cancer and the darkness of death. As a result, even her memory is a source of strength for her children as well as for me.

Perhaps there are times when all parents are concerned about leaving their children behind when they face the dawning of death. Many parents refuse to travel together on long trips for fear that both may be taken at the same time. We should not be reckless, but we should believe that the Bible teaches and remember what we know as we deal with the prospect of death. Through God's *Grace for Dying*, he tells us to trust him. He is our strength. He is taking care of us. He will provide for our children.

"Fear not; [there is nothing to fear] for I am with you; do not look around you in terror *and* be dismayed, for I am your God. I will strengthen *and* harden you [to difficulties]; yes, I will help you; yes, I will hold you up *and* retain you with My *victorious* right hand of rightness *and* justice" (Isa. 41:10).

Bitterness, dread, fear, anxiety, and hysteria about death can destroy our witness for God. It matters not who dies or how important a person is to us, life must and does go on. The key to remember is that God makes adequate provision for every believer concerning physical death. Of course, we will miss a friend or loved one who has died. Death is a separation and is always mentally painful for those left behind. But through faith in our position in Christ, we can go on living with confidence and peace of mind when death invades our family circle. It is important to remember that God has a purpose for us in life as long as we are physically alive. However, that plan is realized only through the ministry of the Holy Spirit in our everyday lives. We must relax into God's grace-provisions—then the death of a loved one or a friend will not hinder God's purpose.

So often we may harbor regrets about how we have treated someone who has died. This is a useless mental attitude. As believers in Christ, we are to turn every regret over to the Lord and move on. To move on is to keep trusting in God and his Word.

4. Another proof of God's preparing us for death is that God takes us home at the right time.

This is often misunderstood. The issue is not old age. When a Spirit-controlled believer dies, young or old, he is of a full age. On the other hand, when a believer logs more time in carnality than he does in spirituality, he may shorten his days on earth. The point is that God's time to take us home is the *right* time. God does not promise a ripe old age. Rather, he promises that as we allow him to be King in our lives, when he does take us, we will have lived a full life. "You shall come to your grave in ripe old age, and as a shock of grain grows up [to the threshing floor] in its season" (Job 5:26).

The human way to think of a full life is in terms of a ripe old age. But God doesn't measure our lives by the number of years we live. Furthermore, we shouldn't question God's wisdom. Elderly people often become bitter and vicious. Then, when we see a person die in their prime, we may say, "the good die young." But the Word of God clears our thinking at this point. When God takes a believer home, he knows exactly when to do so. God has a purpose for every life and when he takes a spiritual believer, whether he is young or old, it is at the right time. First Corinthians 15:55 teaches that the sting has been taken out of death, and the grave has been robbed of its victory. "O death, where is your victory? O death, where is your sting?" (1 Cor. 15:55).

The Participation with God

With God's protection and preparation concerning life and death, whether we live or die, we are participating with God. All through this lifetime, living is an adventure with God for the believer. Thus, we cooperate with him through faith, we will not only enjoy living, but we will also be prepared for dying.

Our participation with God will be successful as we become

saturated with the Scriptures and celebrate Christ consistently under the Holy Spirit's control. This can be accomplished as we acknowledge God's availability and adequacy and confess all known sins moment by moment. In addition, when we are not mindful of any mental-attitude sins, sins of the tongue, or overt sins, we are to constantly cooperate with Christ in daily dependence. This can be realized as we celebrate our relationship with him through genuine thanksgiving. One great attitude which we can use is to acknowledge God's presence in us.

Summary

1. God's *Grace for Dying* involves each situation and set of circumstances we will ever face in this lifetime.
2. Successfully coping with every vexation and the Bible information about God and heaven, as well as the awareness of his deliverance in extreme difficulties, can be major avenues for God to prepare us for both life and death.
3. As we allow God to provide abundant living, we can experience his peace of mind and comfort in the face of extreme dangers and adversities.
4. The Holy Spirit can indoctrinate us with the confidence and mental stability which operates beyond human understanding (Phil. 4:6–7).
5. When we think about death from God's perspective, we can know that our lives cannot be terminated by death.
6. Our faith in God's protection, based on his essence, and his preparation through the intake of Bible knowledge under the Holy Spirit's control is the key to mental victory and assurance.
7. As a result, we can consider life and death as a fantastic participation with God.
8. From this God-given perspective, death need no longer be considered a monster or a fatal enemy.
9. Rather, we can relax and know that death is but a doorway through which God can take us to be with him forever (John 14:3).

8
The Time for Dying

We have recorded the reality of God's *Grace for Dying* before death comes. Now we will consider God's grace-provisions for our actual encounter with death. Every person has an appointment with death, some early in life and others later. Our time of dying may be over an extended period or of a very short duration. In either case, God provides his written Word and his personal presence as our source of confidence and courage. His mental stability is available regardless of the manner of life we have lived, the kind of death we die, or the suffering involved.

The Blessedness

Every believer can be relaxed about death because he has the blessedness of God's presence abiding in him in the person of the Holy Spirit. This blessed happiness is often expressed just prior to the sudden death of a young or middle-aged person. Because he indicates a profound happiness, those who remain often call his death a tragedy. Yet, this happiness and the expression of it can be the blessedness of dying grace which the Lord provides through his grace package.

In the case of prolonged suffering, *Grace for Dying* is provided in a somewhat different way. The believer, as he or she endures the pain, can become a delightful demonstration for the Lord's mercy. During the death experience, they usually experience alternating periods of great happiness and mental peace in the midst of the pain. Furthermore, in the face of death, they will fail to evidence extreme fear, unreasonable concern, or panic. They are possessed by a rational stability with the anticipation of death rather than a morbid dread. They often indicate that they are looking forward to moving into fullness with God.

The believer who dies over a long period of time is provided with such fantastic grace-provisions that his dying can be one of the most productive phases of his life. Then when death comes, there may be a smile just before the last breath is taken. There could be a comment about seeing a great light. The name of Jesus might be uttered. No matter what the circumstances, the believer can be relaxed about death. God's *Grace for Dying* can provide great comfort for those left behind.

A Beneficiary

Another dimension of God's *Grace for Dying* deals with suffering. Here we can realize that whatever suffering we may have to endure, we are its beneficiaries.

The Reasons for Suffering

Why is there so much suffering? In spite of the difficulty in deciding on an answer, the Bible declares that we are not destined to deal with suffering alone. Through his grace, God has provided his perfect provisions for every type of suffering that we can face.

(1) Suffering may come as a result of poor health. Something may go wrong with the human body which results in physical pain and suffering.

(2) People can cause us to suffer, and we may cause them to suffer. We all have a negative anti-God principle in our minds. Many negative attitudes may be manifested, such as gossip, slander, jealousy, and fighting. These are some of the avenues whereby people can cause one another to suffer.

(3) Another source of suffering can be the lack of the basic biological, mental, and emotional needs required to function in the world. Some of these needs might be food, shelter, water, friends, or in some cases, a marriage partner.

(4) The weather can cause us much suffering as it expresses itself in violent storms, extreme heat, or unbearable cold.

(5) Mental and emotional problems such as anguish, worry, anxiety, and the anticipation of something that may never happen can cause us to suffer. For example, some can suffer long and hard anticipating a life outside of marriage, or the seemingly gloomy prospects of widowhood.

(6) Many suffer because of the laws of God, as well as the laws of the land. When we violate God's spiritual laws which govern our relationship with him, we come under his discipline. Also, when we violate the laws of the land and get caught, we may suffer from the system of human justice. Even if we manage to avoid punishment, we must still face God's justice.

(7) Perhaps our greatest source of suffering comes when we seek to handle a situation apart from God's control. In any area of responsibility, where we attempt to operate on our own, we can experience either mental, emotional, or physical suffering.

The Purpose in Suffering

As we relax into the Holy Spirit's control and fill our minds with Bible principles, we can learn that God brings blessings out of all kinds of suffering.

(1) Suffering can teach us obedience, just as it taught Jesus obedience to endure the cross for us in his true humanity. "Although He was a Son, He learned [active, special] obedience through what He suffered" (Heb. 5:8). For so many, it takes suffering to bring them to the realization that they must depend totally on God for everything.

(2) Suffering can test and develop our faith. Adversity can make our faith in God stronger as we learn and live on Bible promises. "Moreover—let us also be full of joy now! Let us exult *and* triumph in our troubles *and* rejoice in our sufferings, knowing that pressure *and* affliction *and* hardship produce patient *and* unswerving endurance" (Rom. 5:3).

God is not in the process of making us strong enough to handle our own problems. We are always weak. God makes our faith stronger as we feed his written Word to the indwelling living Word. Through testing our faith, God can teach us to keep on trusting him regardless of the situation. Many times it requires suffering to bring us to that yieldedness which allows the Holy Spirit to produce his fruit in and through us. In this way God's power is demonstrated in and through our suffering (1 Pet. 1:7–8).

(3) Witnessing for Christ is often made more effective through suffering. With the Holy Spirit operating freely in our lives, we become an open letter for all who cross our pathway to read. "You show *and* make obvious that you are a letter from Christ delivered by

us, not written with ink but with [the] Spirit of [the] living God, not on tablets of stone but on tablets of human hearts" (2 Cor. 3:3).

(4) Through suffering, God attempts to teach the unbeliever to give the gospel a hearing, to repent, and to wake up spiritually. God doesn't wish for anyone to spend eternity in separation from him. Many times it is through suffering that God can bring an unbeliever to a positive volition toward him.

(5) There are times when we will suffer for the sole purpose of allowing God to bring glory to himself. All the suffering of the believer in this lifetime can become one of God's avenues for blessing. Even when we are out of fellowship and living in carnality, God can use discipline in order to bring us to confession. At the point of confession, the Holy Spirit brings us back into fellowship with God. And even though the scars may remain, the suffering becomes a blessing, and God is glorified.

(6) Furthermore, God may use our suffering to illustrate some great doctrinal truth. We will not experience suffering in heaven. It is only during this lifetime that God has the opportunity to reveal himself through suffering.

(7) One of the greatest benefits of our suffering may be to help others who suffer. Through our sufferings, God can teach others that he is sufficient for all the heartaches of life.

In general, suffering is a constant reminder that God's power is available and adequate for all the pressures of life. In each area of life, we can find no greater solace than the strength he can give as we turn to him in total surrender. Fortunate is the person who practices dependence on God in everything. God is our source of stability. He can provide the proper mental attitude upon which we can function in the experiences of suffering and in our encounter with death.

We have the solution to every area of suffering through God's presence within us in the person of the Holy Spirit. The key is to know that we belong to him. He will neither leave us nor forsake us. Knowing this, we can be occupied by God's power and presence rather than the fear and finality of death. So we are not alone in suffering, nor has God forsaken us at the moment of death. We cannot be defeated. Every day will be a victorious day because we are operating on what we know about God. This mental approach to life makes us a beneficiary of suffering and death rather than their victim.

A Bridge

We have indicated that at the time of dying, God's grace provides the blessedness of his personal presence and makes us the beneficiaries of any suffering we may be required to endure. In addition, we have a bridge of adjustment called *grief*.

The Reality of Grief

To many the area of grief is one of the great setbacks encountered in relationship with dying.

(1) Evidences of grief. After the initial shock of death, grief may be evidenced by physical, mental, and emotional symptoms. Some physical manifestations might be queasiness in the stomach, sharp pain, pounding or throbbing in the head, a cottony sensation in the mouth, palpitation of the heart, and disorientation to our surroundings. Mental symptoms may be evidenced by constant sighing, an empty feeling, the loss of appetite, the fog of unreality, talking too much, and lack of memory in routine affairs. Parallel to these physical and mental reactions are emotional symptoms such as stress, the drastic change in normal habits, highly agitated patterns of activity, and idealizing or even refusal to talk.

(2) Dealing with grief. In dealing with grief, a loved one may attempt to preserve the illusion of the deceased's presence. For several months, he may set the table for each meal with an empty plate. The deceased's clothes might be laid out and his room kept the same as it was before death. On the other hand, there could be an attempt to avoid all evidence of the deceased. Pictures and clothing and personal effects could be destroyed. The loved one might move to another house or even to a new geographical location.

There are those who talk to the picture of the person or even talk to them at the grave. A bereaved person can become so mentally intense with this pattern that he may imagine the actual physical presence of the deceased in the room.

(3) Guilt feelings. Another factor in the grief process is guilt feelings. The loved ones can plague their minds with such thoughts as, "If something had been done sooner," "If I had only thought," "If I had been more understanding," "If I hadn't left her alone," "I should never have argued," "If he could only come back so I could tell him

how sorry I am," "I wish I'd been nicer to her." In attempting to deal with the agony of guilt feelings, varied reactions might occur. Some might make elaborate funeral arrangements. Guilt can drive a bereaved person to spend foolishly on the funeral. In an attempt to quiet guilt feelings, some may feel forced to give large sums of money to a charity or to their church as a peace offering.

(4) The hostility of grief. It can express itself against the doctor, the nurse, a relative, or even the deceased's mate. Sometimes the pastor or the funeral director can become the target of such attempts to live with the loss of a loved one. Furthermore, the hostility could be directed to the deceased. Such complaints might be, "Why did you die and leave me alone to raise these children?" A bereaved person may flex his fist in anger against God, seeking some valid reason for the disease or the accident which caused such an upheaval in his life-style.

Grief can become very destructive when we move into overactivity, or take on the symptoms of the illness or the despondency of the deceased. Another danger signal might be total withdrawal from social relationships.

Thus, every bereaved person has to deal with the distraction of grief. But God can use this normal emotion as a bridge of adjustment for those who are left behind. Even in our encounter with the grief syndrome, God's grace is adequate.

God Uses Grief

The psychic pain and frustration of death is real. For a time after the death of a loved one, our world will seem wrecked. Since grief is a natural reaction to death, we must learn to live with it logically. Many are indoctrinated to keep their expressions of grief quiet. Cultural demands, community expectations, and group mores can cause us to deny normal reactions and to observe death in unrealistic ways. We may feel that people and even God expect us to keep up a certain image as we encounter death. But this attitude is wrong, because it can short-circuit the ministry of grief. Let us look at some of the ways God can use grief to lead us through our adjustment to death.

(1) The expression of tears. Following the shock of death, we may face great pressures. One God-given method to release them can be through the shedding of tears. Ironically, one pressure we may

encounter can come from the idea that a Christian shouldn't cry when bereaved. We may try to lock up our tears inside. We may use diversions to more delightful things, or we may try to forsake our feelings in an attempt to avoid tears. We may refuse to let our minds relax into the reality of what is happening. But these approaches seldom meet with success, and they deny a perfectly normal, God-given emotional response.

If this confining of tears continues, we may experience an emotional blowup which could not only be embarrassing but also erosive to our own well-being. Actually, we must not be ashamed of our tears, nor are we to grovel in guilt because of them.

The shedding of tears will not only serve to relieve our grief but it can also release us from much mental and emotional pressure which is related to death. As we build our lives on Bible knowledge and yield to the Holy Spirit's control, the shedding of tears will not get out of hand and become hysteria.

(2) Grief takes time. After the loved one has gone, there may be times when everything seems to stand still. In most cases there is a slowness about grief. Its process is never pushy. However, this can be one of the major ministries of grief's goodness. Grief's passive pace is really a provision of God's *Grace for Dying*.

So, we can relax and remember that this slowness is the normal timetable of the grief syndrome. There are those who invariably attempt to resist grief's gradualness. They may rush religiously back to their old routines. Now, there is some value in keeping busy physically. But if we do not relax mentally, this can be a mistake. We can rob ourselves of grief's healthy healing.

It is right not to rush into some of the normal routines of life. For example, if your mate has died, it would be wise to wait awhile before becoming seriously involved with another of the opposite sex. Also, it would be advisable to allow at least a year to elapse before remarriage. Time is an added asset in the restoration of our mental and emotional capacities to become involved successfully in another marital relationship.

We must cooperate with God in the grief experience because it has to work its way out of our systems. For some, this may include a few weeks in the hospital where we can rest physically, emotionally, and mentally. Because we are believers, we have the opportunity to get the sorrow out of our systems in such a way that God is glorified. We can allow God's healing processes to work, and soon many of the fears and dreads associated with the experience of death will disappear. One great aid in adjusting to the slowness of grief is to commit to memory Bible promises and principles and then to think them throughout the day and night.

Consequently, the slowness of grief can be encouraging and enlightening for the believer who walks by means of the Holy Spirit and wants God's Word.

(3) Grief hinders our energy. When death penetrates our personal world, it drastically disrupts our life-styles and schedules. Yet, life must go on, and decisions must be made. In the process, we may discover a definite ebbing of energy. Our minds, emotions, and wills may register zero. We may deliberately delay making decisions about anything. In many regular routines, everything will seem useless.

Situations which usually pose no problems can take on major proportions. Even though the bills are paid, the weather pleasant, and friends rally round us, we can experience deep lows and anguish. We may appear to be in a mental fog. We may find it necessary to make a superhuman effort just to get through the day.

As we face this energy fallout, we will need special attention from our loved ones and friends. At this point, friends and relatives should be alert to move in and do what is needed, rather than asking what can be done. Prayer and Bible-based discernment can help as we seek to be an avenue of blessing to those who are bereaved.

(4) Grief levels our pride. Death is an effective equalizer. The grief experience can level our pride because when it comes to death, we go the way of all mankind. This realization is usually an unpleasant realization. But this is good for us as we move mentally through the adjustment to death. It can result in mental and emotional growth as we admit that we have no place to turn but to God. If we fail to zero in on God and his promises, loneliness usually sets in.

We may feel alone even in a crowd. If we will remember what we know about God, we can be alone *without being lonely*. Also, during this period, it would be to our advantage to fill our time with wholesome, constructive activities. The realization that we, too, need help can also teach us how to express true empathy. Furthermore, it can allow the Holy Spirit to build in our minds the capacity to be a vehicle of God's love to others.

(5) Grief can be considered a grace-provision from God. We see that God can use grief to bless us. In fact, once we begin to relax into the Holy Spirit's control, we are well on our way to the proper adjustment concerning life and death. With the Holy Spirit's ministry throughout the grief experience, we can move back into our world of routines with this wholesome restoration. We can arise from our battle with bereavement, having achieved assurance and confidence. The key is an attitude of cooperation with the Holy Spirit through faith. This faith-rest is facilitated by him as we zero in on God's promises.

Suggestions

Since the grief syndrome is a vital part of our adjustment relating to death, here are some suggestions that may help you in dealing with death.

(1) Remember what you know about God moment by moment and situation by situation.

(2) Praise the Lord consistently. Let the things you know about heaven control your mind. Think often on the truth that one day you will go to heaven. Refuse to spend time wrestling in worry about things here on earth. Instead, faith-rest everything. That is, ask the Holy Spirit to control your thinking as you cope with each one. The more we know about heaven, the less important the pressures and pleasures of this life will be, and we will keep our priorities in order. As a result, we will be more than conquerors. Since heaven is so marvelous, we shouldn't be reluctant about going there. Tremendous power can be released in our thinking through consistently praising the Lord.

(3) Allow God to minister to you. Through faith in the fact of God's Word, we can experience his love and comfort. Jesus refers to physical death as "sleep." When a person dies, there is a sense in which his physical *light* goes out, and his *eternal light* takes over. Forevermore we are released into *total healing*, free to enjoy life with God. Through God's *Word*, we can glean these principles and realize that this present body is a perishable container. Once we are released from it, we are alive and well in heaven. Remember, if healing doesn't take place in this lifetime, it will the moment we go to heaven!

(4) Celebrate your relationship with God every day. When a believer dies, it is a time of sorrow for the loved ones because death always means separation. But it can also be a time of joy and celebration. We can rejoice that the deceased is enjoying a perfect new life secure in his or her eternal home. We can celebrate the fact that God is preparing us for death every day by teaching us how to live by grace through faith. We can celebrate the truth that God is able to impart supernatural strength which assures us of victory in the midst of any pain or suffering. It is essential to celebrate life every day. It is such a great witness to others. Those who cross our pathways will be impressed when they see our positive reactions to difficulties and pressures. Through genuine celebration, an inner mental attitude of beauty can emerge, which nullifies any evidence of a sour spirit.

(5) Confront the sorrow and separation on the basis of God's grace-provisions. Orientation to God's grace can cause us to think of our going to heaven as God's special coronation service for us personally.

(6) Stay busy but avoid a rigid schedule. In this concept, refuse to be too hard on yourself. Through the control of the Holy Spirit, you can learn to be patient with yourself. Take time to appreciate the loved ones and friends who are still with you. Give yourself plenty of breathing room to take in Bible doctrines and think them without ceasing.

(7) Spend time alone. During these periods, we can mentally look forward to the time when we shall be with our loved ones in heaven. If our deceased loved one or friend was an unbeliever, we can know that their loss of heaven will not hinder our joy. We will not be aware of them when we are in heaven. God has made us with the capacity to adjust. Those in heaven will not be concerned with any suffering present on earth or in hell.

(8) Search for ways to minister to others. You can pray for others who face bereavement. You can visit them, send cards, or write letters of encouragement. There are always avenues of ministry to others for the Spirit-controlled believer. The result for you will be the by-product of inner happiness and mental peace.

(9) Make a memory notebook. So often, some make the mistake of trying to shut out all memory of their loved one who has died. One way they try to do this is to remove all evidence of the loved one from

the house. A Spirit-controlled, Bible-oriented believer may want to keep a memory notebook of all sorts of things which relate to the loved one. There will be sympathy cards, letters, and pictures. He can include personal articles which once belonged to the deceased. Notes and gifts, which can be a source of fantastic comfort as well as pleasant remembrances, could be included.

(10) Live on a crash program of Bible doctrine intake. At the time of our encounter with death, we usually find ourselves focusing mentally on heaven. In the meantime, we are confronted with the pain and sorrow of the separation. We must then deal with grief effectively. God's grace-provisions provide Bible promises as a means of setting us free from superficial means of coping. As we acknowledge God's presence in our minds and take time to learn Bible promises, we will be surprised how we can move forward in our personal lives.

These are just a few suggestions which can help us build a mental bridge of adjustment through the grief syndrome and over that intermission between earth and heaven called death. Remember, if our loved ones are with Jesus and Jesus is in us in the person of the Holy Spirit, our loved ones cannot be too far away spiritually. Remember, the sorrows that we experience here in this lifetime are small compared to the joy of heaven.

Summary

1. At the time of dying, God's grace provides the blessedness of his personal presence and makes us beneficiaries of any suffering, real or imaginary, which we may be requested to endure.
2. God's *Grace for Dying* builds a spiritual bridge which enables the Holy Spirit to make our transition into eternity a smooth one.
3. God's presence and power are available for us at the time of dying.
4. He is our strength and sufficiency for living and dying.
5. We are not compelled to be alarmed about death because God doesn't forsake us nor does he ever leave us alone.
6. Once we allow God to establish a relationship with us, death is really no longer our enemy.
7. The believer can think soundly about death regardless of how or when or where it strikes.
8. This is true because God's joy and peace of mind are available in every aspect of our encounter with death.

Part V
Grace for Eternity

As we come to the last division in God's garden of grace-provisions we discover a *Living Hope* concerning our relationship with that spiritual world beyond physical death. We shall refer to this area as *Grace for Eternity*. This concept of God's grace includes all that he has planned and will provide for us in eternity. Our emphasis will be centered in "Absent from the Body, Present with the Lord," and "All Things New."

9

Absent from the Body, Present with the Lord

Life on earth begins with physical birth, and is terminated by physical death. But death is not the end of our existence. Every believer and unbeliever will live beyond death for all eternity. Much investigation and speculation on life beyond death is available. But reason, faith, and the Scriptures speak of definite survival beyond death and of our future resurrection. God created mankind to live forever and every person will do so. Therefore, the issue is not life after death, but our destination. There are two possible states of existence for mankind beyond death: separation from God, hell, or personal relationship with God, heaven. Each person has free will and decides which state he will abide in forever.

Although we are limited in detailed knowledge and firsthand experience concerning life's other side, God's grace-provisions can enlighten us sufficiently. Through Bible information, we can experience great confidence, exercise genuine commitment, and evidence gratifying celebration in our anticipation of death.

Confidence

Because of Adam's disobedience, sin invaded man's relationship with God, resulting first in spiritual death which eventually led to physical death. From the moment sin entered the human race, everything and everyone began to decay and die. The Hebrew of Genesis 2:17 reveals that God told Adam, "In the day thou eatest thereof [dying], thou shalt surely die" (KJV). The *first* dying is the spiritual death which is separation from God. This breakdown in relationship with God began back before the foundation of the world when Lucifer the archangel rose up in rebellion against God. It occured in the human race when Adam disobeyed God. As a result, all of Adam's descendants, the entire human race, inherited spiritual and physical death. "Therefore as sin came into the world through one man and death as the result of sin, so death spread to all men [no one being able to stop it *or* to escape its power], because all men sinned" (Rom. 5:12).

Therefore, every person is born into the world cut off from a personal relationship with God. The *second* dying mentioned in Genesis 2:17 is the physical death which occurred in Adam several hundred years later. The truth that all humanity dies physically is positive evidence that all men are spiritually dead. Thus, death came on the scene as a result of sin. Every person is born into the world spiritually dead. His destiny is to be eternally separated from God. Furthermore, in no way could mankind resolve this separation from God. This was accomplished by God through his work of grace on the cross. Jesus' death on the cross and his resurrection from the dead provided for us the possibility to change our future abode. This means that every person can exchange separation from God for relationship with God. However, this change of destiny has to take place during this lifetime. There is no scriptural evidence for the concept of repentance beyond the grave.

The exchange was accomplished at our moment of salvation by the Holy Spirit. He moved into our lives, performed the spiritual birth, placed us in union with Christ, and established an eternal relationship with God. These basic theological doctrines can be a source of great confidence as we orient to them. Death is never entirely welcomed. However, for the believer its power to enslave with fear can be neutralized because Jesus' view of death destroys its fearsome aspects.

Jesus' View of Death

Jesus' teachings concerning death were revolutionary. He conquered death; and through our faith-relationship with him, we also conquer death. In Mark 5:39 Jesus referred to death as being asleep. He deliberately used this metaphorical language to teach us in terms we could relate with. Here, he meant the ceasing of the activities of life in relationship with others on this earth.

In John 11:1–45, we have the story of the raising of Lazarus. In this context, Jesus presented his conception of death as something which brought mental quietness and rest. He related that death is not a monster to be feared. Also, Jesus regarded death as having secondary importance to a life of faith dependence on God the Father. He taught that the quality of life which we possess in him was of more concern than death. He recognized the place of birth and death as a vital part of life. But the quality of life between the two was much more important. His thrust was that the believer should zero in on his relationship of life with God. It is through properly learning how to live that we can cope successfully with every aspect of death.

Paul's View of Death

Another source of confidence concerning death is found in Paul's teachings. He used some of Jesus' metaphorical terminology, and implied specifically that the departure of the believer from this lifetime meant immediate presence and fellowship with the Lord. "[Yes] we have confident *and* hopeful courage, and are well-pleased rather to be away from home out of the body and be at home with the Lord" (2 Cor. 5:8).

Romans 5:12 and following indicates that death was introduced into the world by sin. Therefore, the presence of death was positive evidence of the presence of sin. Paul considered death as the penalty of sin. Paul also taught that through faith in Jesus Christ, the believer has victory over this penalty called death. By grace through faith, death becomes an entrance into blessedness with God. Paul said that the time is coming when both sin and death will be subjugated to God's power. Therefore, while alive here on earth, we can have mental-attitude victory over every encounter with death itself as we live by faith in Jesus Christ and believe what the Bible teaches about life beyond death. Thus, after death we will gain the reality of Jesus' complete victory as we move into the personal presence of God.

In Romans 8:10 the body is subject to death but the soul and spirit are not. Also, in God's own time we will receive a new resurrection body which will not be subject to death. In 2 Timothy 1:10, Paul further taught the truth that Jesus has destroyed death and brought forth life and immortality. In his perfect purpose and plan, Jesus absolutely alienated death. But the reality of victory has not yet been consummated. It will be realized in eternity after death. In the meantime, we are to reckon as true our victory in Jesus and keep on trusting him. Remember, faith has to be based on established criterion. The truth of our victory over death has been established. Our responsibility is to believe it even though its reality has not been fully realized. As a result of our faith in the facts presented in the written Word, the indwelling Holy Spirit will make it a mental reality.

In Hebrews 2:14–15, we are told by the writer that the devil can use death as a club over us. But Jesus Christ removed the club from Satan's power. Then in Philippians 1:21–23, Paul related that for himself to die would be his gain. He expressed the idea that to die meant departing from this life and being with Christ forever. This prospect was better for him than to continue on earth with all the pressure and hardships.

Furthermore, Paul believed that since God gave him a body for his spirit and soul during this lifetime, he would also do the same in the next life. In the meantime, Paul saw that to depart this life meant that he would move into a disembodied state and enjoy the fullness of God. Then the time would come when he would receive a resurrection body.

Paul related that death would be a crowning event for him (2 Tim. 4:6–8). He had lived a life of faithful service to God. He had fought the good fight of faith. He had finished his course in this life. Paul realized that his physical life was behind him. There was no turning back. However, death was not the end. Before him, death provided a great doorway. Paul's knowledge about God gave him the proper perspective about this doorway. It meant pleasant prospects ahead. He was more than a conqueror. Death would not defeat him. It meant a glorious victory.

In Revelation 14:13, death is presented as a desirable adventure for the believer. We have a living hope. "Praised (honored, blessed be) the God and Father of our Lord Jesus Christ, the Messiah! By His boundless mercy we have been born again to an ever living hope through the resurrection of Jesus Christ from the dead" (1 Pet. 1:3). Thus, from the divine perspective, we can face *Absence from the Body, Present with the Lord* with absolute confidence because of what we know about God.

Commitment

Death is the cessation of life as the spirit and soul depart the body whether by natural or violent means. After death, the unbeliever will be in the state of conscious punishment forever. The believer will be in a state of perfect blessedness forever. Since the physical body has served its purpose, it is laid aside. Then the body decomposes. The chemicals and gases return to the earth.

On this side of death, anticipating the future can be gloomy for anyone who is negative to God and his written Word. Death will seem to stalk us as its prey. Thus, its appearance can be dark and foreboding, and its uncertainty can make it a dreaded enemy. If we are lacking in our awareness of God, we may consider death as an unfair intruder. It will be that unique finality which cuts us off from the enjoyment of this life. We can actually find ourselves slaves to our fears about death.

However, our commitment to God during this lifetime allows God to prepare us for death, sustain us at death, and escort us through the experience of death. Furthermore, through Bible information, we can learn some principles about our future life which can help solidify our commitment.

First, there is the idea of the disembodied state for both the believer and the unbeliever. This will be the phase of our eternal existence between our physical death and the receiving of our resurrection bodies. This state is not to be considered as a holding place or a halfway plateau.

Second, the disembodied state is to be considered an interim or temporary condition in which the believer will be conscious and enjoying heaven to the fullest. As for the unbeliever, he will exist forever in the conscious state of suffering and separation from God. The provision of the resurrection body is a completion of God's plan for the believer and unbeliever. It will also be a body which can survive the destruction of the universe. The believer will receive his resurrection body at the rapture of the church as he becomes a part of the bride of Christ. This is the first resurrection. The unbeliever will receive his resurrection body at the final judgment as he is sentenced to eternal separation from God. This is the second resurrection.

Third, both heaven and hell are fixed states. Once we move through death our destinies are set for all eternity. The destination we will enjoy in eternity will be decided by our relationship with Christ while we live in time. We can sum up the destination of the unbeliever as separation from God in a disembodied state awaiting a resurrection body at the final judgment. It is a fixed place with a gulf which makes it impossible ever to leave. This means that all the blessings of heaven are denied the unbeliever forever. They will be alive and conscious in the place of eternal punishment.

For the believer, he will be with God in a disembodied state awaiting his resurrection body. Heaven is also a fixed place with a joy which can be no greater (Luke 16:19–31).

Celebration

There are many biblical principles related to the death of the believer. Each one can give us some tremendous reasons to celebrate our relationship with God. These doctrines can be called the *content of our hope* which informs us of what we can expect in heaven.

From modern-day terminology, *hope* is wishful thinking. It is something indefinite, which we may desire but doubt seriously that we will ever achieve. But hope in the Bible is the basic concept which relates to eternity. It means assurance and confidence, a prospect on which we can rely. Thus, the content of our hope is one of our grace reasons to celebrate our relationship with God.

Face to Face with the Lord

After we die physically, we will be with the Lord forever. "[Yes] we have confident *and* hopeful courage, and are well-pleased rather to be away from home out of the body and be at home with the Lord" (2 Cor. 5:8).

No matter what we are as believers, carnal, spiritual, immature or mature, the moment we die we will be face to face with the Lord. Thus, we should never be overly disturbed by dying or death. The manner of our death is in the Lord's hands. We will move "through the valley of the shadow of death" and on the other side we will be face to face with the Lord.

All Sorrow Removed

In eternity, all regrets, tears, and sorrow will be terminated for the believer. Some project the idea that we will not be happy in heaven if we fail to accomplish certain works for God while here on earth. They may indicate that when the judgment comes God will parade all of our sins out in the open before everyone to make us ashamed. This is ludicrous. In reality, believers will not be present at the final judgment (Rev. 20:11–15). Others say that God will make us grovel in misery for our lack of service or failure to support some church program. These ideas are legalistic, man-made gimmicks to manipulate people. They may cause emotional response during an invitation, but they can be a disgrace to God.

Now it is true that every believer has to face the judgment seat of Christ in eternity. "For we must all appear *and* be revealed as we are before the judgment seat of Christ, so that each one may receive [his pay] according to what he has done in the body, whether good or evil, [considering what his purpose and motive have been, and what he has achieved, been busy with and given himself and his attention to accomplishing]" (2 Cor. 5:10). But this is an emphasis on the production of the believer during this lifetime. Basically, it is God's assessment of the believers in which all human production and the sin nature are eradicated. In addition, we will be rewarded on the basis of what we allowed God to do in and through us during this lifetime.

In 1 Corinthians 3:11–16, the wood, hay, and stubble refer to deeds done in our own strength. The gold, silver, and precious stones refer to the deeds and ministries we can do under the Holy Spirit's control.

Remember, death is a doorway into a place where there never again will be any kind of pain. "God will wipe away every tear from their eyes, and death shall be no more, neither shall there be anguish—sorrow and mourning—nor grief nor pain any more; for the old conditions *and* the former order of things have passed away" (Rev. 21:4).

No Judgment

"Therefore [there is] now no condemnation—no adjudging of wrong—for those who are in Christ Jesus, *who live not after the dictates of the flesh, but after the dictates of the spirit*" (Rom 8:1). In Hebrews 9:27, "It is appointed unto men once to die, but after this the judgment" (KJV). However, for the believer this judgment is eliminated. "I assure you, most solemnly I tell you, the person whose ears are open to My words—who listens to My message—and believes *and* trusts in *and* clings to *and* relies on Him Who sent Me has (possesses now) eternal life. And he does not come into judgment—

does not incur sentence of judgment, will not come under condemnation—but he already has passed over out of death into life" (John 5:24).

This means that God will never judge us because his righteousness was transferred to our lives the moment we received Christ as Savior.

An Eternal Inheritance

"[Born anew] into an inheritance which is beyond the reach of change *and* decay (imperishable) unsullied, and unfading, reserved in heaven for you" (1 Pet. 1:4).

This inheritance can be anticipated with great joy. God is preserving it for us. Furthermore, he will take care of us and make sure we get to heaven to receive all that his *Grace for Eternity* provides. Thus, we share all that Christ has for all eternity. Since no one in heaven will have a sin nature, there will be no struggle for status. Nor will there be any pressure of jealousy or complaining of another being favored by God.

An Eternal Home of Security

"And when (if) I go and make ready a place for you, I will come back again and will take you to Myself, that where I am you will be also" (John 14:3).

At death we go home to be with God. We will live in God's mansions which he has prepared. If a believer is unaware of this concept, he may anticipate death reluctantly. The thought of a homeless eternity can be very frightening. But the Bible teaches us that such fears are groundless. We have God's assurance of an adequate dwelling place prepared by Jesus for his people. Whenever we die, God will be ready for us.

No Anti-God Principle in Our Thinking

On the other side of death, the sin nature or self-life will be eradicated from the believer's mind. "There shall no longer exist there anything that is accursed—detestable, foul, offensive, impure, hateful or horrible" (Rev. 22:3).

All that we have done under the sin nature's control, "wood, hay, and stubble," will be destroyed. There will be no sign of the anti-God sin nature in heaven. All human production will be gone. Furthermore, all we have done in the power of the Holy Spirit will remain. This production is referred to as "gold, silver, and precious stones," which will form the basis for our rewards in eternity.

It seems to disturb some people that even though a believer logs most of his time in carnality, he is still rewarded for those few times when he is controlled by the Holy Spirit. This is not a license to sin, but freedom to live.

A Resurrection Body

"Who will transform *and* fashion anew the body of our humiliation to conform to *and* be like the body of His glory *and* majesty, by exerting that power which enables Him even to subject everything to Himself" (Phil. 3:21).

At the rapture, the believers who have already died will receive their resurrection bodies. Jesus will bring them with him to the atmosphere around the earth. "For since we believe that Jesus died and rose again, even so God will also bring with Him through Jesus those who have fallen asleep [in death]" (1 Thess. 4:14). At the same time, all believers here on earth will be changed into resurrection bodies and will be taken out of the world to meet the Lord in the air (1 Cor. 15:51–52).

First Corinthians 15:39–50 deals with the characteristics of this resurrection body with the figure of a seed. Paul said the body is planted like a seed. Just as the seed dies and a new body emerges, so in the resurrection there will be a resurrection body of a higher order of existence. Then he uses several contrasts to explain what our resurrection will be like.

(1) "Sown in corruption; . . . raised in incorruption" (KJV). Here, the physical body is subject to decay. This will not be true of the spiritual body in heaven.

(2) "Sown in dishonour, . . . raised in glory" (KJV). The physical body is planted in dishonor because of the defiling presence of the sin nature. But the resurrected body will be raised a glorious body. It will in no way be defiled by the sin nature or any sins.

(3) "Sown in weakness; . . . raised in power" (KJV). Here on earth, the physical body is limited and handicapped in some way. It can never measure up to the potential of God's plan and purpose. In eternity, our resurrection bodies will be free of all limitations or

handicaps.

(4) "Sown a natural body; . . . raised a spiritual body" (KJV). This is the main issue of what Paul taught regarding the essence of the resurrection body. Paul insisted that the believer will have a body in heaven (vv. 44–49). It will be a spiritual body. Just as the earthly body is perfectly fitted to the needs of the physical plan, the heavenly body will be perfectly suited to the spiritual plan of existence.

In summary, our resurrection body will be perfect in every way. It will never get sick. There will be no decay of any kind. It will not be hindered by any physical obstructions, nor will there be any limitations of time or space. Time is for our advantage in this lifetime, but will not be necessary for eternity. As we investigate, in detail, the Scriptures which deal with life beyond death, most of the references to angelic bodies, such as Jesus' body and the believer's resurrection body involves light. The major concepts seem to indicate that light will be a definite part of our resurrection bodies.

Therefore, because of God's grace-provisions, even though our physical lives will end at physical death, because we are born again, we will have an everlasting life which can never end. This wonderful quality of spiritual life guarantees that our relationship with God will last forever. God the Father planned it. God the Son executed it on the cross. God the Holy Spirit established it through our faith and the intake of Bible knowledge. The entire Trinity sustains and perpetuates it forever.

Summary

1. Absent from the body, face to face with the Lord can be an adventure for every believer.
2. When physical death takes place, our bodies are vacated and will remain on earth.
3. Our soul and spirit will be immediately in the presence of God in a disembodied state.
4. During this lifetime if we are born only once, the physical birth, we will die twice, the physical and spiritual death.
5. However, if during this lifetime we are born twice, the physical birth and the spiritual birth, we will die only once—the physical death.
6. Therefore, the physical death is not the end of our existence, but

rather, a brand-new beginning of an existence on an entirely new plain.

7. From the moment of the believer's death, he will enjoy heaven to its fullest.

8. At the rapture of the church from the earth, all believers will receive a resurrection body.

10
All Things New

We have studied Paul's premise that at death we go directly to be with the Lord forever. We can be aware of God's assurance and adequacy *now* about our future life. As the concluding chapter of our earthly lives ends, we begin an entirely new script in heaven. We can face our personal pressures and problems with an undefeatable positive attitude. Those enlightening truths can excite, in our minds, great encouragement to keep on trusting God. Now let's center our thoughts about God's grace-package around the words: separation, security, and service.

Separation

Death always involves some kind of separation. So it is of value to understand the several ways the term death is used in the Bible.

1. In Ephesians 2:1, we are told about *spiritual death.*

In essence, spiritual death is separation from God. It means no relationship or fellowship with God. Everyone begins his pilgrimage on earth spiritually dead. The reason we are born physically alive but spiritually dead is because we have that intruder called the negative sin nature. Remember, once a child reaches the age of accountability, he is responsible for his lost condition and must be born again. We are not spiritually dead because we commit sins. We commit sins because we have a free will and the strong influence of a sin nature which renders us spiritually dead. "And you [He made alive], when you were dead [slain] by [your] trespasses and sins" (Eph. 2:1).

2. The Bible also talks about a *second death* in Hebrews 9:27.

This is a reference to the last judgment of the unbelievers at the end of the world. This is where the unbeliever is separated from God forever and confined to hell. One major reason for this Great White Throne Judgment is because God is a gentleman. His grace-provisions, based on his perfect character, demand that he show the unbeliever why he is refused entrance into heaven. Since the unbeliever has rejected Jesus as personal Savior, he is compelled to rely on his own deeds, philosophy, and ethics as a means of appeasing God. But his efforts are not only in vain and unrewarding, they serve as a basis for divine judgment (Rev. 20:11–15).

3. The term *death* is also used as *failing to be a vehicle of divine production*. "For as the human body apart from the spirit is lifeless, so faith apart from [its] works of obedience is also dead" (Jas. 2:26).

This is faith separated from works. As we live by faith on the basis of Bible principles, the Holy Spirit will produce Christlikeness in and through our behavior. This is that divine good which results from faith in the fact of God's Word. As a result of the Holy Spirit's control, all that we become involved in will be the divine work that pleases God.

In essence, under the Holy Spirit's control, he does the producing through us. We become the vehicle of God's work. On the other hand, when we fail to allow the Holy Spirit to control our minds and bodies, the sin nature controls. As a result, all we can do will be our own human efforts, which can't please God (Isa. 64:6).

4. Then there are references to *identification with Christ in his death*. "For [as far as this world is concerned] you have died, and your [new, real] life is hid with Christ in God. When Christ Who is our life appears, then you also will appear with Him in (the splendor of His) glory" (Col. 3:3–4). This kind of death is separation *from* spiritual death. The believer is dead in Christ, which means to be positioned forever in him by means of the Holy Spirit.

"And He raised us up together with Him and made us sit down together—giving us joint seating with Him—in the heavenly sphere [by virtue of our being] in Christ Jesus, the Messiah, the Anointed One" (Eph. 2:6). Our position in Christ implies eternal security. We can never lose our salvation. This is not a license to sin but freedom to live a grace-oriented life.

5. Romans 8:6,13 are references to death as being *carnal*. "Now the mind of the flesh [which is sense and reason without the Holy Spirit] is death—death that comprises all the miseries arising from sin, both here and hereafter. But the mind of the (Holy) Spirit is life and soul-peace [both now and forever]" (Rom. 8:6).

Carnality indicates that even though we are positioned in Christ forever, we can be out of temporal fellowship with God. This means to be controlled by the sin nature and thus separated from the Holy Spirit's control. Under this concept of death, even though we are still heaven-bound, we are under God's discipline, an ineffective witness for Jesus, a miserable Christian, and unable to pray. Furthermore, we will imitate unbelievers. This negative condition will continue until we confess our sins and once more relax into God's control (1 John 1:9).

6. In Romans 4:16–21, we learn about Abraham's inability to produce offspring. This is a reference to *sexual death*. It means a separation from the capacity to conceive children in natural birth.

7. The reference to death which we are majoring on in *Grace for Dying* and *Grace for Eternity* is *physical death*.

"And just as it is important for [all] men once to die and after that the [certain] judgment" (Heb. 9:27).

Every person is familiar with this kind of death, at least in principle. Physical death is our spirit and soul's separation from the physical body. This means that the body is no longer occupied.

Based on sound Bible doctrine, there is no need for some of the mechanics of modern funerals. When a person has departed this life, he cannot attend his own funeral. The one funeral that we cannot attend will be our own. The only way for a person to be in a funeral home, ride in a funeral wagon, or lie in a casket or even a grave, is to do so while they are still alive physically. "[Yes] we have confident *and* hopeful courage, and are well-pleased rather to be away from our home out of the body and be at home with the Lord" (2 Cor. 5:8).

It is not necessary for the believer to be obsessed about preserving his dead physical body. In fact, we can hinder our witness for Jesus when we make a great to-do over the physical body. Some well-meaning believers are more faithful in visiting the grave of a loved one than in prayer, Bible study, and at times, even church attendance. Open caskets and the viewing of the deceased's body can become an unwarranted mental and emotional drain on those left behind.

As a minister, I have often regretted the undue pressure and hardships which funeral traditions can place on those with whom I sorrow. In many cases, some of these traditions and unscriptural practices can quench the comfort which only the Holy Spirit can give, and they neutralize much of the strength which can come only from the Scriptures.

Based on Bible principles, a Christian funeral should not condone any practices which serve to undermine the availability and adequacy of God's grace-provisions. But many families are uninformed and not grounded in the Bible. They can become slaves to many traditions, just as the unbeliever. Instead of using God's grace-provisions to meet their needs, so many believers rely on the same superficial substitutes as used by those who never honor God.

Here are some suggestions about funerals which would be more in keeping with the principles of God's Word.

First, once a person has died, he could be taken to the funeral home, prepared, and immediately buried apart from any personal contact with the family or loved ones. Of course, funeral arrangements would have to be made. There would be no graveside gathering, unoccupied body to view, or a casket to open. This approach would be consistent with Bible principles because the real person is no longer in the physical body. The moment we are absent from the body, we are present with the Lord. Therefore, there is little advantage and a great deal of expense in all that is involved in going from the church or the funeral home to the graveside.

Second, instead of a funeral service, we could have a memorial and praise service. There would be no sitting around the funeral home one or two nights with an open casket. Some think that this is needed to help the family adjust emotionally in saying good-bye to their loved one. However, any real adjustment during these times depends on the relationship between the family and loved ones and their understanding of the Bible.

These funeral wakes often become a time of partying and reunion for loved ones while the immediate family becomes physically exhausted. They are forced to endure the emotional and mental drain which comes from sitting for hours in the same room with a dead body. They may not have learned or accepted the truth that the body of their loved one is unoccupied.

Too, there is the possibility of serious guilt or mental anguish if the loved ones recall unwholesome circumstances and misunderstandings which may have existed in their relationship with the deceased.

Of course, there are advantages and some needs are met in observing some of the traditions. But it is often at the expense of honor and praise to God.

Many of our funeral traditions can cause serious mental and emotional problems because of certain customs, ways of dress, and conduct which are expected of the bereaved. The better way would be to establish the tradition of having a memorial service on behalf of the departed dead based on praise to God. In this manner, we could not only honor God in a worshipful atmosphere, but we would receive the inner strength and personal comfort which the indwelling, living Word could render through use of the written Word.

This kind of memorial and praise service could take many forms depending on the desires of those involved. The thrust would be on Jesus Christ and his grace-provisions for life and death. Much emphasis could be placed on the living Hope, on Bible promises, and on the principles of grace. The use of victorious music and poetry could bring great comfort. Testimonies from those who have faced death could be implemented.

Third, after the memorial and praise service, there could be a reception in a place large enough to accommodate the family and friends, preferably in the same place where the service is held. At this reception, loved ones and friends could gather to rejoice with the immediate family. The thrust of the celebration would center around the victory the deceased has experienced and will enjoy forever. This reception could replace the traditional funeral wake and give opportunity for loved ones and friends to be strengthened on the basis of God's grace-provisions. Food and refreshments could be served if desired. The reception could be structured to lend to a relaxed, informal atmosphere.

Security

Yes, there is great separation related to physical death and God's grace-provisions can provide the mental stability needed for successful coping. However, immediately after our death, there will be the realization of the eternal security which we have possessed since our moment of salvation. In Revelation 21:3–5, there are three words which indicate the wonderful security we will enjoy in heaven. Actually, this is the only description given in the Bible relating to what heaven will be like. Many use the description of the eternal Jerusalem in Revelation 21:10–27 as a picture of heaven. However, it is more accurate to accept these passages as a description of the headquarters of heaven rather than the entire concept of heaven. The general description of heaven is as follows:

1. *Heaven is the personal presence of Jesus.* "Then I heard a mighty voice from the throne *and* I perceived its distinct words, saying, See! The abode of God is with men, and He will live (encamp, tent) among them, and they shall be His people and God shall personally be with them and be their God" (Rev. 21:3).

The concept of the tabernacle of God refers to Jesus Christ. The idea presented is that in heaven he will be accessible to all in a way not found in this lifetime. Here in this lifetime, we relate to him through the indwelling Holy Spirit and the written Word. Based on the tabernacle concept under the principle of the Shekinah glory, the resurrection body of Jesus contains light. Since our resurrection bodies will be like his, we will contain light. Perhaps recognition of one another in heaven will be based on having some kind of indwelling light.

2. *Heaven is perfect happiness.* "God will wipe away every tear from their eyes and death shall be no more, neither shall there be anguish—sorrow and mourning—nor grief nor pain any more; for the old conditions *and* the former order of things have passed away" (Rev. 21:4).

The reference to tears relates to pressures and sorrows. The things which cause these kinds of tears will be removed. First, death is removed. On earth the anticipation of death is often the source of human tears. When there is severe pain or continuous suffering, we may immediately associate it with the possibility of death. But in heaven there will be no death to be the source of fear and anxiety.

Second, sorrow will be removed. This is a reference to mental agony or pain. In heaven there will be no mental agony or pain to cause sorrow. Third, crying is removed. Crying is a manifestation of pain. In heaven there will be no crying caused by pain. Fourth, pain is removed. This is a reference to physical pain. Therefore, former things are passed away.

3. *Heaven is perpetual newness.* "And He Who is seated on the throne said, See! I make all things new" (Rev. 21:5). Here on earth,

there is perpetual decay in the midst of restoration. During this lifetime, many of our concerns must be related to restoring and replacing most of the details of life. However, in heaven nothing will ever get old. This perpetual newness is based on God's faithfulness.

These three characteristics will be the eternal status quo of the believer forever. The believer is linked to an eternity with God from the moment of salvation. This relationship which is established in this lifetime will continue in heaven forever. The entire package of grace for eternity depends totally upon God's perfect character. Anything which comes from God is absolute and reflects his glory.

Service

During this lifetime, it is often asked, "What will we do in heaven?" The scriptural answer is the simple statement, "We will serve God."

"For this reason they are [now] before the [very] throne of God, and serve Him day and night in Him (temple) sanctuary; and He Who is sitting upon the throne will protect *and* spread His tabernacle over *and* shelter them with His presence" (Rev. 7:15).

It is interesting to note that the thrust in heaven will not be on our work for God, but rather on what he will be able to accomplish on our behalf. In Revelation 7:15–17, we are told that God, "shall dwell among [us]" (KJV). This means that God will spread his tabernacle or protection among us. His presence will protect us. We will never again hunger or thirst. No longer will the sun or anything burn us. Jesus will have no hindrances in being our Shepherd. For all eternity, he will be able to guide us, supply our every need, and give us perfect joy.

It is enlightening to see that the same thrust which will characterize our relationship with God in heaven shall also dominate our fellowship with him here on earth. God has designed our lives on earth to center on what he provides for us and what he can accomplish in and through us. From the grace-perspective, it is not what we do for God that counts, but what we allow him to do in and through us. The major hindrance to this grace-orientation in our lifetime is our self-life perpetuated by the sin nature. Unless there is maximum Bible doctrine and the filling of the Holy Spirit, we will tend to place the emphasis on what we can do to earn or deserve our salvation and God's *Grace for Living* (and death).

As we relate to our service in eternity, we must understand the concepts of rewards and crowns. The Bible indicates that there will be some type of rewards for us in heaven. The rewards will be based on our service as avenues of divine production. This would mean that when we allow the Holy Spirit to control us, whatever God accomplishes in and through our lives will be the basis of rewards.

Whatever the nature of our rewards, evidently they will relate to crowns. It seems that we will lay these crowns at Jesus' feet. This could mean that regardless of the characteristics of rewards, they will not be for our own status, rank, or position. Here on earth we associate rewards with our own personal edification. But in heaven, rewards will be a wonderful way to serve Jesus effectively. We can better understand this concept as we study the Bible and what it teaches about crowns.

In 1 Corinthians 9:20, the *incorruptible crown* (KJV) is mentioned. This reveals that the nature of our rewards will be spiritual. They will never fade or perish. In James 1:12 and Revelation 2:10, the *crown of life* (KJV) is introduced. This concept is that sin's temptations and terrific testings will come. Yet, if we remain occupied with Christ, we will reap the deeply satisfying life which God has designed for us.

Then in Philippians 4:1 and 1 Thessalonians 2:19, Paul spoke of the *crown of joy* (KJV). This is a reference to believers who live and think by grace, master the details of life, relate to others with a relaxed mental attitude, and learn the capacity to love. The believer with this *Greater Grace* life-style shall enjoy the spiritual penthouse of happiness for all eternity. In 2 Timothy 4:7–8, the *crown of righteousness* is emphasized. This refers to believers who operate on the principle of faith-rest, using God's righteousness as their absolute standard. The two principles to remember are that crowns are a result of spending time in fellowship with God under the Holy Spirit's control and that crowns relate to our willing service to God by grace through faith.

Summary

1. The Christian life is divided into living and dying.
2. Whether our dying is sudden or of a long duration, it does not rob us of eternal life.
3. Also, we can have happiness and evidence a wonderful testimony regardless of any suffering which may be related to our dying.

4. As we learn to live on the basis of grace, and as we faith-rest everything, any fear or anxiety about death is neutralized.
5. We will enjoy God's *Grace for Dying*, regardless of the kind of Christian life we have lived.
6. Regardless of the circumstances involved in dying, the believer can relax, knowing that he is dealing with God.
7. Because of Christ's work on the cross, every believer has a relationship with God that death cannot destroy.

Principles for Daily Living

Life can become an "overcoming adventure" as we relax and rejoice in the grace of God. This faith attitude frees God the Holy to accomplish his fantastic ministry in and through our lives. Perhaps the greatest thing that God does for us through his grace-provisions is to fashion us to be like his Son—Jesus Christ. He accomplishes this in a threefold manner.

1. At the time of our salvation, we are born again.

At the moment of salvation, the Holy Spirit places us in union with Christ. We are identified with him forever. This is our position of eternal security which can never be changed. Thus, we should always remember our position in Christ.

God's grace-plan to make us like his Son began for us at the moment of salvation, when the Holy Spirit placed us in union with Christ forever.

"For those whom He foreknew—of whom He was aware and loved beforehand—He also destined from the beginning (foreordaining them) to be molded into the image of His Son [and share inwardly His likeness], that He might become the first-born among many brethren.

And those whom He foreordained He also called; and those whom He called He also justified—acquitted, made righteous, putting them into right standing with Himself. And those whom He justified He also glorified—raising them to a heavenly dignity and condition [state of being]" (Rom. 8:29–30).

2. In the second place, during our experiential life on earth, God makes us like his Son as he uses us for the purpose for which we are designed: that is, to bring glory to himself.

Glory means to picture what God is like. As we function under the Holy Spirit's control, God can meet every need and pour out superabundant blessings. As we yield in availability and release the Holy Spirit to control us, he expresses the life of Jesus in and through our lives. Just as Jesus was available to God the Father, we are to be available to the Holy Spirit as vehicles of his love. The more we live under the Holy Spirit's control, the more we become avenues of Christlikeness wherever we go. "As you have therefore received the Christ, [even] Jesus the Lord, [so] walk—regulate your lives *and* conduct yourselves—in union with *and* conformity to Him" (Col. 2:6).

3. *In eternity we will be complete in Jesus with resurrection bodies void of a sin nature.*

God the Father will have free access to our lives. There will be no rival to quench and grieve him. He will be able to do all that he has prepared and planned for us.

The point is that we are ambassadors for Christ. We represent him, not by what we do for him, but in our availability as avenues of his grace-provisions. Furthermore, God is just waiting to give his *Grace for Salvation* to the unbeliever, and to release his grace-provisions for living and dying in and through every believer.

But grace-provisions do not guarantee automatic peace and happiness. God's peace and happiness are only a potential and are realized only when we are controlled by the Holy Spirit. One of the benefits of Spirit-controlled living is that, as the pressures and problems of life touch our lives, we are stabilized by the Holy Spirit. So they can't hurt or get to us in a destructive way. Each time the negative influence of mental-attitude sins hits us, we can admit our total dependence on God and relax mentally into his control. The Holy Spirit will then take the Bible truth which we have learned and use it to stabilize us mentally.

God is waiting to give us guidance, to deliver us, to defend us, and to relax us mentally. In addition, God desires to pour out in each of our lives many of his grace-provisions, promotions, and prosperity as we have the capacity to receive them. Grace is not what we earn or deserve. Grace is all that God can do for us because of Christ's death on the cross. From our knowledge of God's provisions, we can derive some principle to remember before, during, and after every routine, responsibility, and relationship.

1. The *power of God* in the life of the believer is the source of the *peace of God* for every confrontation.
2. All that God has provided for humanity is available to the person who is available to all that God has provided.
3. It takes God's power released in us in order to be the person God intended us to be.
4. Our greatest availability to God's adequacy begins with availability to Bible knowledge.
5. We can wake up every morning knowing that we already have a good day ahead of us, regardless of what happens—because of what we know about God.
6. Every day can be an exciting adventure for the person who is born again and knows the reality of being controlled by the Holy Spirit.
7. Every day can be a super-grace day, and every experience can result in superabundant living as we learn to faith-rest into the Holy Spirit's control and live on the basis of Bible principles.
8. One of the greatest lessons we can learn in this lifetime is how to love people from the grace-perspective.
9. God's love is not a feeling but a right mental attitude which sets our thinking straight, accomplishes the job of Christian living, and is minus such negative attitudes as hate, worry, fear, and revenge.
10. The Christian life is a relationship with God which depends totally and absolutely on his perfect character, whereby his life is related to our lives through our response of faith.
11. Our witness for Christ is the *activity* of God *revealed* in our behavior which results from the life of God being *released* in our thinking through our faith in the fact of God's Word.
12. The Christian life is always present tense. It is not what happened in the past or what we hope will happen in the future. It's what's happening right now.
13. Axiom for grace. Grace is God's unmerited favor. Grace is God's package of provisions provided for our profit. Grace is God's wealth and wisdom waiting for willing minds to want. Grace is Christ's mind wrapped in his written Word. Grace gives us the right to have what we don't deserve. Grace is all of God's

activities of love poured out for our benefit because of Christ's death on the cross and resurrection from the dead.

14. Faith is counting what God promises as true and waiting on his time of revelation.

15. Faith takes what God's grace offers and says, Thank you, Father.

16. God is not interested in the promises we make to him, but in our positive faith-attitude toward his promises to us.

17. God is not in the business of making us strong enough to handle our own problems. We are weak and always will be. God's purpose is to make our faith in him stronger so we depend more and more on him. This is accomplished as we feed the written Word to the indwelling, living Word—the Holy Spirit.

18. God has made adequate provisions for every problem, pressure, heartache, and crisis which we will ever face.

19. Faith-rest is the key to releasing the Holy Spirit to control our thinking. Faith-rest means to turn it over to the Lord or to put it in God's hands, wait on the Lord. These idioms mean that because we put our faith in the fact of God's Word, we can allow the Holy Spirit to control our thinking as we face a problem or any situation.

20. God's solution to every problem begins with providing the mental stability needed to cope with each situation which arises. Then, if we encounter favorable circumstances or situations which go against us, we will be able to make the proper adjustment.

21. Instead of trying to get it all together, we should relax, and let God put it all together for us. Our responsibility is to stop messing up our lives and hindering God's working in and through our lives. As we discover God's grace-provisions as our *Reason for Joy*, God will be able to use us for the purpose for which we were created—to be a vehicle of glory to him. As a result, we share everything which Christ has. We share such things as his priesthood. We have direct access to God. We share his kingship. We will reign with him forever in eternity, and we also reign with him during this lifetime, when we are controlled by the Holy Spirit. We also share his heirship, his sonship, his election, his destiny, and his inheritance forever!